Advance Praise for *Nea.*

"Open-hearted and soulful, never morbid, and often uplifting, *Near the Exit* is a colorful travelogue of mortality. I've read many books on illness and dying; few have made me smile as often and see the uniquely human richness of the final chapters of life."

—Ira Byock, author of *Dying Well* and *The Best Care Possible* and Active Emeritus Professor of Medicine, the Geisel School of Medicine at Dartmouth

"*Near the Exit* is a delicious, funny, and quite moving read. Part *actual* travelogue, it's also a *spiritual* exploration of death. The writing is stellar; the reflections on the unexpected nature of grief and the way Lori Erickson plumbs 'seeming coincidence' grabbed my attention and didn't let it go. Highly recommend for people of any or no faith practice."

—Jennifer Grant, author of *Love You More* and *Maybe I Can Love My Neighbor Too*

"Erickson is our expert tour guide as she takes us on a colorful journey of the world's sacred death rituals and destinations. Her vivid prose is our companion and invitation to the spiritual packing we needn't delay until the night before departure."

—J. Dana Trent, author of *Dessert First: Preparing for Death While Savoring Life*

"*Near the Exit* is not a typical book on death and dying from a Christian perspective. It is an intriguing exploration of late life and death that will sometimes cause you to squirm or to laugh out loud. Always though, it will prompt you to think deeply about what it is to be mortal. Author Lori Erikson fearlessly weaves ancient perspectives and cultural expressions about death gleaned from her own travel experiences into the intimate stories of her mother's life in a nursing home in Iowa. *Near the Exit* will appeal to anyone who struggles to understand the mystery of death and dying."

—Missy Buchanan, advocate, writer, and speaker for older adults

"What happens when a gifted travel writer combines her interests in travel, religion, and death? The result is a fascinating book called *Near the Exit*, with trips to Rome, a Day of the Dead celebration, pyramids in Egypt and Mexico, nursing homes, a Maori ceremony in New Zealand, a farm in Iowa, and more. Beautiful writing about a trip we all will someday take."

—Brian D. McLaren, author and activist

"When I first picked up *Near the Exit*, I found that, much to my relief, I had not commenced to read another grief book. Instead it's a travelogue that explores a wide range of sacred sites—from the exotic (and musty) pyramids of Egypt's Valley of the Kings to the Iowa nursing home where Lori's elderly mother navigates the labyrinth of dementia—all characterized by a light-hearted and curious inquiry about what death means in various cultural and spiritual contexts.

As one who has been hanging out with the Grim Reaper more than I care to lately, I took this book in like a breath of fresh air. I hope *Near the Exit* will help others navigate mortality as Lori Erickson meets us wherever we are and gently invites us on a guided global tour."

— Kate Sheehan Roach, Director of
Content, ContemplativeLife.org

"Is it possible to become comfortable with the thought of one's own death? Lori Erickson sets out on a fantastic voyage to explore the answer, and, best of all, we get to go with her. From the depths of Egypt's Great Pyramids to the wide-open spiritual expanse that is Crestone, Colorado, *Near the Exit* shows us that it is possible not only to chart the landscape of mortality but also to make it gloriously our own. A hopeful and inspiring book."

—Sophfronia Scott, author of *This Child of Faith:
Raising a Spiritual Child in a Secular World*

Near the Exit

Also by Lori Erickson

Holy Rover: Journeys in Search of Mystery, Miracles, and God

Near the Exit

Travels with the
Not-So-Grim Reaper

Lori Erickson

WESTMINSTER
JOHN KNOX PRESS
LOUISVILLE • KENTUCKY

© 2019 Lori Erickson

First edition
Published by Westminster John Knox Press
Louisville, Kentucky

19 20 21 22 23 24 25 26 27 28—10 9 8 7 6 5 4 3 2 1

Book design by Drew Stevens
Cover design by designpointinc.com

Library of Congress Cataloging-in-Publication Data is on file
at the Library of Congress, Washington, D.C.

ISBN-13: 9780664265670

PRINTED IN THE UNITED STATES OF AMERICA

∞ The paper used in this publication meets the minimum requirements
of the American National Standard for Information Sciences—Permanence of Paper
for Printed Library Materials, ANSI Z39.48-1992

For the Ericksons—Myron, Grace, Alan, and Carl

Contents

At Chicago's Day of the Dead celebration (PHOTO CREDIT: BOB SESSIONS)

Prologue
A Tutorial in Death

In the Chicago neighborhood of Pilsen, death was everywhere: splayed out on a beach towel like a vacationer who'd gotten way too much sun, dressed in a spangled tuxedo as it walked on stilts through the crowd, projected as a huge dancing skeleton on the side of a building.

I'd come to the National Museum of Mexican Art to attend the largest annual Day of the Dead celebration in the United States. I knew that on the first two days of November in Mexico, people honor their deceased loved ones with celebratory visits to graveyards and home altars set with pictures, foods, and flowers. During Día de los Muertos—All Saints' Day and All Souls' Day on the Christian calendar—the dead are said to return for a visit. Chicago, with its large Mexican population, is one of a growing number of cities that have claimed the celebration as their own.

After parking our car, my husband, Bob, and I passed through an open area next to the museum that held decorated altars, some set up on tables and others placed on the ground. A shrine topped by a photo of an older man holding a violin caught my eye, especially when I saw it was tended by a woman wearing a black dress adorned with a skeleton that made her look like she was wearing a portable X-ray machine. Painted stitches crisscrossed her lips and her face was deathly white with black eye sockets, but she also had a perky red heart on her chin and flowers and ribbons braided into her hair.

When I asked about the man commemorated on the altar, she was eager to talk. Her grandfather had been a talented violinist, she said, and then told me about the significance of the other items on display—the vinyl records he'd listened to, the foods he'd enjoyed, a picture of the '72 Mustang he'd loved. At the center of the altar was a crucifix resting against her grandfather's violin. I felt like I knew him, just from seeing the tokens and symbols arranged with such care on the table.

A few feet away, another altar included a more unusual item.

"Is that a condom?" I whispered to Bob.

The woman standing by the table overheard my question. "After my son died in a car accident, we found that condom in his wallet," she explained. "We're proud of him for being so responsible."

She was happy to talk to us, too, telling us about her son's academic successes and his love for his nieces and nephews. We admired his baseball cap, an arrangement of his favorite candy bars, a soccer ball he'd once kicked around the neighborhood, and pictures of him with his teammates.

As we ventured farther into the aisles of altars, I saw images of the Virgin Mary and Jesus, but much older traditions were visible as well, harking back to pre-Columbian indigenous beliefs. The hollow eyes of masks stared at me, the faces marked with symbols I didn't recognize. Decorated skulls made of sugar were common, along with the round loaves topped with sculpted bones known as *pan de muerto*, the bread of the dead. Many altars had skeleton figures arranged in scenes from everyday life, from playing guitars and riding bicycles to dancing in ball gowns. Marigolds were everywhere, and I remembered reading that their color and strong smell are said to help the dead find the altars.

A long line of people waiting to enter the museum snaked around the corner and extended for several city blocks, while near the outdoor altars others waited to have their faces painted, often with the pallor of death covering just one side. In their somber black clothes adorned with skeleton motifs, many of them looked like they were on a date with the Grim Reaper. But the whole scene also had a wholesome air about it, as families and friends socialized and chatted with strangers who had questions about their altars.

As night fell, I struggled to make sense of the sensory overload. While I'd known a little about this festival before arriving, nothing prepared me for the sheer weirdness of it. This was *death* people were honoring, satirizing, and embracing. I'd been taught that dying is solemn and sad, best kept confined to funerals and cemeteries and spoken of in hushed voices. But in Pilsen death was everywhere, though not in its typical depressing form. Instead the Grim Reaper was having a good time, here at the Day of the Dead.

I'd come to this festival after a summer of loss—my mother's entry into a nursing home with dementia, followed four days later by the sudden death of my fifty-nine-year-old brother from a heart attack. I was still trying to recover from other losses as well, including the deaths of several close friends. And I was beginning to realize that this loss thing isn't going to get any easier. I'm of an age when I attend two funerals for every wedding. I buy sympathy cards in bulk, and when I stand at the checkout counter, watching as the clerk totals them up, I wonder what names I'll be writing on the envelopes.

In the midst of my melancholy, the Day of the Dead was a burst of brilliant color. I'd been drawn here, I realized, because I needed a tutorial in death. I didn't need to know about the stages of grief or how to make a living will; I needed to know how to *live* with death. This festival blending death, whimsy, and remembrance was a beginning. It made me want to learn more about what it meant to invite the dead to come back, and then bid them leave again.

I've long been curious about death. In high school, the results of a career interest inventory indicated that I was uniquely suited to being either a teacher or a funeral director. When I ended up being a writer instead, one of my first projects was a collection of ghost stories from my corner of Iowa, a book that taught me that if Iowans do come back as ghosts, they're a lot like they are in life—friendly, helpful, and low-key, the sort of spirits who are more interested in rearranging furniture than spattering blood on the walls or tripping people at the top of the stairs.

Here's another qualification I have for writing a book about death: I'm going to die. I don't want to be rude, but you are too. And I think this fact is worth pondering before we get to the point where we aren't buying green bananas any longer.

One of my most important lessons on death came from a comment made by Franciscan priest and author Richard Rohr after a speech. He was asked by an audience member, a man who worked in a hospice, why he thought so many people have such a difficult time coming to terms with their deaths.

"Well, you don't want to leave your spiritual homework until the night before the test," Rohr replied.

I've had that as a cautionary principle ever since. I don't want to be the student who has to pull an all-nighter before glory beckons, trying to cram in all I should've learned along the way.

Every religion tries to help its followers deal with death: it's one of the Big Questions that few of us can avoid contemplating. We can easily skip over the parts of the exam relating to phenomenology and hermeneutics, but the ones on death are not in the extra-credit section.

My own religion, Christianity, says that when we die, we're resurrected in Christ. I believe this with all my heart. I don't know how it happens, exactly, but I'm on board with all of it. I think we will rise on the last day, healed and whole, and that God will wipe away the tears from every eye, to use words from the book of Revelation, that text better known for its scary verses than its comforting ones. And I love that dreamy, gauzy picture that depicts Jesus on a cloud, embracing a man who's just arrived in heaven. This is how it will be, I think, after I breathe my last.

Because theological consistency has never been my strong suit, on many days I also believe in reincarnation. I think that maybe we go to Jesus when we die, and after a nice rest we return to this plane of existence for another ride on the merry-go-round. In my next life, I hope to have a beautiful singing voice, a preference I occasionally mention aloud just to keep it on the divine radar.

I've come to believe that the boundary between life and death is more porous than many of us realize. I've felt this in places around the world, in quiet churches where beams of sunlight slanted across the pews, on beaches where it seemed as if I could walk across the water to eternity, in prehistoric stone circles that hinted of a portal to another world, and in cemeteries where I was ready to purchase a plot just to be able to soak up the serenity in perpetuity.

This book is about places that have helped me come to terms with death, sites that have made me view it not with dread but with acceptance, and even a measure of comfort and curiosity. Some of these locations require a plane ticket—the Valley of the Kings in Egypt, for example, and the Vatican Necropolis in Rome. But I also ponder more universal destinations, including nursing homes, funerals, and graveyards.

I realize this subject has been well plumbed by people much more learned and wiser than me (Plato, King Solomon, C. S. Lewis, and Tolstoy, among others I count as my spiritual and literary betters). And however eloquent and profound our ruminations may be, we just don't know, do we? Perhaps at the end of our lives we'll end up in a parallel universe where we'll get the chance to live our lives backward.

But I do know this: birth comes with a free ticket giving us permission to speculate on death and what, if anything, comes after. We don't need a theological or medical degree for these ruminations, just human DNA. As far as we know, we're the only creatures that have this capacity to anticipate the end of our lives. It's a somewhat mixed blessing, to be sure, but one of endless fascination for many of us.

I have a somewhat-unusual perspective on these matters because I'm both a member of the clergy (a deacon in the Episcopal Church) and a travel writer specializing in holy sites. I know from long experience that my senses are never keener than when I first step foot in new territory—it's one of the reasons, in fact, why a newcomer who's an experienced writer can often convey the customs and nuances of a place better than a native. And as a deacon, I often encounter death, from vigils in hospitals and the administering of last rites to the planning of funerals. So in this book I try to blend these two perspectives. I approach the ordinary venues where death touches our lives as if they're travel destinations, and I visit bucket-list locales with my figurative clerical collar on. What are the social customs of a nursing home or a graveyard? What spiritual lessons can be learned inside the Great Pyramid? And what can the Aztecs, those enthusiastic practitioners of human sacrifice, teach us about death?

I've found that lessons about mortality are nearly everywhere, once you start looking for them.

After returning home from Chicago, I set up my own Day of the Dead altar. I began by rummaging through my closet for pictures of loved ones who've died. I chose an image of my brother opening a Christmas present decades ago, a wide smile on his face. My maternal grandmother was next: the photo showed her holding a new grandbaby, her gaze warm and loving. From the other side of my family I picked a photo of my paternal grandfather, an overalls-wearing farmer standing next to a barn. He's tall and thin, his hands worn by a lifetime of labor.

The photo of my parents came next. It's from early in their marriage, more than a decade before I was born. My dad wears a suit, tie, and hat set at a jaunty angle; my mom is wearing a flowered dress and sports a 1940s hairdo. She comes up just a little above his shoulder, and the grins on their faces show that they're crazy in love.

Taking my cue from the altars I'd seen at Day of the Dead, I added other things as well: chocolate, flowers, and a candle. And finally a letter, one from a packet of yellowed epistles we found in my mother's dresser when we cleaned out her house after she went into a nursing home. She'd received these notes from my father when they were courting. I'd been astonished when my sister discovered them, as I had no idea my man-of-few-words father could be so tender and passionate. I put the letter in front of their picture, realizing there were things I didn't know about this couple, despite the many years I'd spent with them.

After arranging each item just so, I lit the candle and sat before the altar, my gaze shifting from one photo to the next, inviting the dead to return to shadowy life, if only for a short while.

I'm visiting my mother in her nursing home, and she's telling me about her difficulties in remembering things.

"If this gets any worse, I may have to go into a nursing home," she says.

We've had this conversation repeatedly over the past few months, one that at first was funny and now is just perplexing. What do I say in return? "Mom, you *are* in a nursing home" seems unkind, as the prospect of going into one doesn't seem to please her. I settle for a weak, "We'll cross that bridge when we come to it, Mom."

She's usually content in her new home, which most of the time she thinks is her former workplace, the food service at the local college. But much has been forgotten. On my last driving trip with her, the one that convinced me she needed to enter a care facility, she couldn't find the doctor's office that she'd visited for twenty years. I don't take her for drives anymore, having been advised by the staff that it would be too confusing for her.

When I call or visit, she frequently talks about the dead as if they're still alive. "Have you seen Tilman or Howard lately?" she asks me, inquiring about her brothers who died decades before.

I realize she's in the Eternal Now, a state reached not through meditation, but through the gradual fraying of the synapses in her brain. When I'm with her, it feels as if time stops for me as well.

We walk down the hallway to the dining area, where the radio plays a soothing melody and a woman sits in a recliner cradling a baby doll wrapped in a blanket. As we pass her, my mother shakes her head and says matter-of-factly, "She doesn't realize that baby is dead."

Like the Day of the Dead festival, being in the nursing home is surreal, and poignant, and amusing, all at the same time. Only this happens not just once a year, but every time I visit.

Image of the Egyptian god Thoth from the Temple of Edfu along the Nile River (PHOTO CREDIT: MICHAEL VENTURA)

1

In the Field of Reeds

Egypt

Being inside one of the Great Pyramids at Giza is a travel experience, like kissing Ireland's Blarney stone, that's better in theory than in actuality. Even though I'm not particularly claustrophobic or germ conscious, both anxieties came roaring to life during my time inside Khafre's Pyramid, the second in size among the three massive monuments that tower in the desert outside Cairo.

Entering a small doorway at its base, I first walked down a sloping shaft, then climbed for long minutes through a narrow passageway that rose ever upward. The air had the unmistakable scent of having been breathed thousands of times by strangers, and with each step I had an increasingly visceral sense of the oppressive weight of stone above me. I tried not to think about the fact that the pyramids were built thousands of years before the advent of building codes.

At last I reached the central chamber, a small, unadorned room with an empty granite sarcophagus. Standing there, trying to take shallow breaths so as not to take in too much of the well-used air, I thought of all the New Age enthusiasts for whom staying overnight in this place would be the fulfillment of a dearly held dream. If I were to do so, powerful tranquilizers would be needed.

After a few minutes of trying unsuccessfully to think deep thoughts, I reversed my steps and headed back outside with relief. Following the mazelike route felt like an enactment of the mythical journey from the underworld to paradise, and when I emerged again into the bright sunlight of the desert I took deep, grateful breaths of fresh air. A tomb is a tomb, I realized, even if it's one of the ancient wonders of the world.

I wandered over to a tour group to eavesdrop as a guide described the tremendous effort it took to construct these pyramids. The largest, the tomb of the pharaoh Khufu, was built by thousands of people laboring over a period of ten to twenty years. Over a base that covers more than thirteen acres, they stacked 2.3 million blocks of stone to a height of 481 feet. For nearly four thousand years, the Great Pyramid was the tallest human-made structure on earth.

The pyramids were, in a sense, resurrection machines, the guide explained. "Their shape allows for maximum exposure to the rays of Ra, the sun god," he said. "All of that power was concentrated on the body of the pharaoh within."

I gazed upward at the tops of the three pyramids, silhouetted against the sky and the dun-colored desert, colossal piles of stone constructed with almost unimaginable labor and expense. So much effort had been put into propelling the three pharaohs into immortality.

I sympathized with their wish: it's just not fair that this Glorious Me will not continue after death. Throughout human history, many people have believed that if they ascribe to the correct doctrine, do the necessary rituals, and pray to the right god, death will be just a blip on the radar, a passageway to something far better. The Egyptians made a giant bet that they'd discovered the right formula.

For a writer fascinated by both death and religion, a visit to Egypt was the equivalent of a slot machine spitting out quarters. Nearly every place I toured had layer upon layer of history, religious significance, and the inimitably Egyptian take on death and the afterlife. And as I embarked on my tutorial in death after that sad summer of loss, memories of Egypt kept resurfacing. I realized that no other civilization has poured so much of its resources into preparing for death and the afterlife as the ancient Egyptians—and they did so with such grandeur, such over-the-top eccentricity and style, that we're still awestruck by what they created.

I visited the country during a period when its tourism industry was booming, shortly before the Egyptian revolution of 2011. During that political upheaval I was transfixed by the news reports being broadcast from sites that I'd recently toured. I'd greatly enjoyed my interactions with the Egyptians I'd met, the guides and shopkeepers who had welcomed me warmly. I wondered how they were faring in the unrest, and I knew that it would be years before their tourism industry, so essential to the nation's economy, would recover.

But it helps to take a long view in Egypt—a very long view. Here's how far back Egypt's history goes: when the Greek historian Herodotus visited the kingdom around 450 BCE, the pyramids had already been around for two thousand years.

As he toured the country in a state of perpetual amazement, Herodotus set the model for countless tourists ever since. He was dazzled by its palaces, temples, and tombs, its strange hieroglyphs that blended writing with pictures, its elaborate process for turning dead bodies into mummies, and its gods and goddesses that he guessed were relatives of the Greek pantheon. And like many visitors in subsequent centuries, upon returning home he wrote effusively about his impressions, further stoking the Greek fascination for Egypt.

Other people visited the country with more than sightseeing in mind. When Alexander the Great conquered Egypt in 332 BCE, he had himself crowned pharaoh (a big attraction was that Egyptian rulers were also divine—a considerable upgrade for a king). After his death, one of his generals founded a dynasty, the Ptolemys, that lasted for three centuries. Julius Caesar viewed Egypt as an irresistible prize as well, especially after Cleopatra had herself rolled up into a carpet and smuggled into his presence. While she probably wasn't as classically beautiful as legend says, she was well educated, intelligent, and seductive. She convinced Caesar to take her side in a dynastic fight against her brother and husband Ptolemy XIII (if you think tracing your genealogy is complicated, just imagine what it was like keeping track of the family tree of the pharaohs, who often married siblings).

After Caesar's assassination, Cleopatra took up with Roman general Mark Antony, who made her life even more interesting. The two arranged for the murder of her sister, were crowned co-rulers of Egypt, and set new standards for excess, from barges drenched in perfume to the founding of their own private club called the Society of Inimitable Lovers. Their time together ended with a bang: a double suicide. For the shocked citizens of Rome who watched the drama unfold at a distance, their lives were the equivalent of a Spanish telenovela. While they worried that Egyptian outlandishness might corrupt their own society, the drama was nevertheless mesmerizing.

The Roman interest in all-things-Egyptian led a succession of emperors to go obelisk hunting, laboriously hauling the stone pillars back to Rome at great expense. One of them still stands in front of St. Peter's Basilica in Rome. The landmark is said to have witnessed the martyrdom of the apostle Peter during the period when it overlooked the circus—the chariot run—of the emperor Caligula. When pilgrims visit the Vatican today, they walk past a monument much older than Christianity, a pillar that's spent as much time with the god Osiris as with Christ.

Napoleon caught Egypt fever when he invaded the country in 1798. He brought with him more than a hundred scientists, scholars, and engineers, who descended upon the country like inquisitive locusts. They created a catalog of Egyptian antiquities, a multivolume publication that ignited a worldwide interest in pharaohs, mummies, tombs, and pyramids.

And then, on a November day in 1922, a British archaeologist named Howard Carter peered into a newly opened tomb in the Valley of the Kings and spied a glint of gold. "Can you see anything?" asked the man standing by his side, Lord Carnarvon, the wealthy aristocrat who was funding the expedition.

"Yes, wonderful things," an amazed Carter replied.

The moment sent Egypt-mania into hyperdrive, because inside was the tomb of King Tutankhamun—a minor boy king, a ruler who during his lifetime barely made a ripple in the broad flow of Egyptian history. But in death, he had the good fortune to do something that no other pharaoh had managed to do: elude grave robbers.

A ROAD MAP TO ETERNITY

As I traveled in Egypt, it amused me to contrast our modern, secular attitude toward death with that of the ancient Egyptians. For many people today, it's not very complicated at all: at some point in the future, hopefully later rather than sooner, we'll breathe our last. Finis. *Sayonara.* Our friends and family might have a gathering at a funeral home, or a scattering of ashes at a beach, but we shouldn't fuss too much about the details.

Even Christians, those of us who believe in Jesus' promise of resurrection, often aren't very confident about the details: "I'll go home to Jesus, somehow. Not sure how that's going to happen, but I'll end up in heaven."

Contrast these fuzzy-around-the-edges views of death and the afterlife with that of the ancient Egyptians. It took them centuries to work out all the details, but eventually they thought they had it all figured out. They recorded the information in texts that were collected into the Egyptian Book of the Dead, though a more accurate translation is the Book of Going Forth by Day. For them, death was just the first step in a long process that led to eternity. Once people breathed their last, their souls (which were thought to be divided into multiple parts, each with a different function) had to pass through twelve gates, one for each hour of the night. Fearsome beasts and deities guarded each entryway and had to be appeased with the proper spells.

If the souls got the incantations right, they arrived at the Hall of Osiris, the god of the underworld—and then the really hard part began.

A test—a kind of SAT of death—came next. Called the Negative Confession, it consisted of a series of thirty-six denials. People would memorize these in preparation for this moment, but in case they forgot (easy to do, given all the hullabaloo of dying and then those fearsome beasts), relatives would tuck a copy between their legs after they died.

Reading the list of propositions, I can imagine myself standing before Osiris. Some of them are pretty easy:

I have not mistreated cattle. (Nope, not me.)

I have not depleted the loaves of the gods. (I wouldn't dream of stealing food from an altar.)

I have not quenched a needed fire. (Not a problem!)

I have not stopped a god in his procession. (Wouldn't dream of it.)

But other statements make me pause, wondering how anyone could answer them in the negative:

I have not known what should not be known.

I have not caused tears.

I have not made anyone suffer.

After these questions, souls needed to give another set of denials to the forty-two beings who assisted Osiris. To the Bone-smasher who comes from Hnes (a place sorely in need of an extra vowel): *I have not told lies. O Fiend who comes from the slaughter-house: I have not committed adultery. O Cave-dweller who comes from the west: I have not sulked.* And then the souls would list the charitable works they'd done during their lifetime.

At the end of these recitations came the hardest test of all. The heart of the deceased was weighed upon a scale balanced by a feather representing Ma'at, the goddess of truth, harmony, and justice. If the heart was too heavy, if it was weighed down by sins and evil deeds, it was thrown aside to be eaten by a demon who was a combination crocodile, lion, and hippopotamus, who no doubt was very well fed, given the many ways people could fail the test.

Or, an alternative doctrine said that the unworthy dead weren't disposed of immediately but instead were banished to a place where they had to walk upside down, drink their own urine, and eat their own excrement. As a final indignity, they even lost their shadows, which were highly valued by Egyptians.

But if people were virtuous, their souls could at last enter the next world, the Field of Reeds, which wasn't so much a paradise as it was a continuation of life in this world, only without any pain and suffering. If people were farmers in this life, they'd be farmers in the next. They'd be reunited with beloved pets and have a home like the one they'd left behind. The afterlife was like this life, only better.

And as if all of this complicated process wasn't hard enough, back in the earthly realm, the person's body had to remain in good enough shape that the soul could still have a home. Otherwise, the entire quest for eternal life was doomed to fail.

The desert gave the Egyptians the idea: its heat and aridity naturally preserved dead bodies, evaporating all their moisture and leaving behind a husk that could last indefinitely. Ironically, the bodies of the wealthy interred in tombs tended to go bad much faster than the poor who were buried in the desert.

Mummification took this natural process a step farther. First, most of the internal organs were removed and put into jars—though not the brain, which the Egyptians thought had no function, and so every trace of it was cleaned out from the skull and thrown away. Spices and other aromatics were put into the body and then it was covered with natron, a mineral salt that removed water from the tissues. After a number of weeks, the corpse was painted with resin, which dried to a hard, impermeable crust, and then wrapped with strips of linen, with amulets tucked inside the folds to provide added protection. All of this seventy-day process was done under the strict supervision of priest-embalmers, who ensured that the proper religious rituals were followed at each step.

Originally only the pharaohs received the full mummy treatment, but the fashion spread to the upper crust, and then filtered downward into society (though the poor still got buried in the desert). By this time, the mummification trade was booming. Various price points were offered, ranging from pull-out-all-the-stops to bargain-basement rates. Animals were also mummified, including cats, dogs, ibises, falcons, baboons, serpents, and even tiny shrews. Some were given as offerings to the gods, and others were likely pets that would be good company in the afterlife.

All of this effort and expense gave people their best shot at having a pleasant eternity. And once the whole industry got started, it lasted for thousands of years.

TREASURES UNDER THE SAND

Building the Great Pyramids turned out to have been a mistake: they were the equivalent of a blinking neon sign saying, "Look for treasure here." Robbers, undeterred by the curses that protected the tombs, stripped them of their riches within a few centuries. Today the pyramids continue their work of harnessing the sun god's power, only all of that energy is focused on empty chambers whose occupants have long since departed.

Realizing that small and hidden was more prudent than big and gaudy, pharaohs began constructing tombs four hundred miles south in the Valley of the Kings near Thebes, now known as Luxor. Over the next five centuries more than sixty tombs were built in this remote desert valley. Since the process of hewing chambers out of limestone took many years, a new one was begun soon after a pharaoh was crowned.

You have to wonder what it was like for the pharaohs as they watched their tombs being constructed, knowing what the entrance fee was going to be. But their belief in the afterlife was likely so strong that they watched it all with approval—observing and inspecting as workers chiseled underground passages beneath the valley floor and then artisans painted elaborate decorations and symbols on their walls, floors, and ceilings. And after they'd breathed their last in their magnificent palaces, their retainers stocked their tombs with all the goods they'd need in eternity, from food, drink, and luxury goods to boxes of small figurines that could be magically transformed into human servants as needed. As a final step, the tomb's inconspicuous entrance was sealed and camouflaged. Nothing to see here, no sirree. Just another jumble of rocks in the desert. The contrast with the Great Pyramids couldn't have been greater.

Unfortunately, grave robbers have remarkable persistence, especially when there's fabulously valuable treasure involved. Eventually the tombs were discovered and stripped of their contents (even King Tut's tomb showed some evidence of tampering, but the thieves left without taking much, perhaps because they were caught in the act).

As I walked up the ramp leading into one of these tombs, I thought of how in centuries past what I was doing would have gotten me killed in a most gruesome way, from being burned alive to impaled. Today it's easy to enter the sacred precincts: I simply bought a ticket, stepped through a door, and headed down a corridor leading into a series of rooms, one after another, each adorned with hieroglyphs and images of gods and goddesses on the walls and ceilings. Hardly a square inch was left unpainted. Because the tombs had been sealed for centuries, the colors were surprisingly bright, the ochres, golds, and midnight blues still bearing the brush marks of their creators. Many of the pictures were of divine beings that blended animal and human forms, from the jackal-headed Anubis to Horus, who has the head of a falcon. The writings, I'd been told by a guide, contained rituals, incantations, and prayers meant to assist the pharaoh on his journey to immortality. And at the center of the tomb stood a carved granite sarcophagus, its mummy long since removed, but still the sacred center of this grand barge of death.

Despite the tourists milling around me, I stood looking at the sarcophagus for quite some time. As much as I admired the cultural and artistic sophistication of the people who'd created it, I didn't believe their story of the journey to the afterlife. But whatever happens after we breathe our last, in Egypt I realized that I share their sense that something more than nothingness awaits us. This desert people may have been wrong in the details—I certainly hoped so, especially that bit about the demon that devours the souls of people who've ever made anyone cry—but the broad outlines of what they believed rang true to me. Along with them, I think that another world awaits us, one of mystery and wonder. And I hoped that the pharaoh who once occupied this granite coffin was now in the Field of Reeds, that land where no sorrow or sickness could find him. With some luck, his shadow was there with him too.

While much of what I saw in Egypt was foreign to me, the longer I toured, the more resonances I found between my world and that of the desert kingdom.

In the Coptic quarter of Cairo, especially, I discovered connections to Judaism and Christianity, places that made me recall the many Bible stories set in Egypt. I learned that Christianity found a receptive home among the Egyptians in the first and second centuries, and that even after Islam came to Egypt in the seventh century, Christians continued to be a vital minority within the country. Today about 10 percent of Egypt's population is Christian, most as members of the Coptic Orthodox Church (a denomination whose name derives from the Greek word for Egyptian). They trace their church's founding to Mark, the apostle who came to Egypt in the middle of the first century.

Here in the oldest part of Cairo, two sites in particular captured my attention. The first was Ben Ezra Synagogue, which legend says was built near the spot where Moses was found as a baby by a daughter of the pharaoh (his mother had put him in a basket and set him afloat on the water in hopes he'd escape the edict that all Hebrew male babies were to be killed). Rebuilt multiple times through the centuries, the synagogue's interior is stately and grand, though it's no longer an active place of worship. Nearby, I visited the Church of Saints Sergius and Bacchus, said to be built on the site where the Holy Family lived after fleeing Bethlehem because of King Herod's search for the baby Jesus. Other than in Jerusalem, I'd never felt so clearly the ancient roots of my Christian faith.

My guide to these sites explained that early Christian missionaries drew on the similarities between existing religious beliefs and the new faith. The stylistic similarities between the ankh, the ancient Egyptian symbol of life, and the Christian cross helped make people more receptive to the message of the Gospels. The Egyptian god Osiris, like Christ, had been betrayed, unjustly killed, and resurrected. His wife, Isis, was frequently shown holding their son Horus, an image that morphed into statues of the Virgin Mary and the baby Jesus (sometimes, in fact, they simply took an Isis statue, did a little touch-up work, and announced that it was now Mary and her son). Both religions taught that death was followed by a time of judgment and then entrance into eternal life. And a belief in the Son of God wasn't that much of a stretch for those who believed that their pharaoh was already a son of god.

In Egypt, I realized that religions, like environmentalists, believe in reusing, repurposing, and recycling.

I thought as well of how our modern world has its own obsessions with immortality. We don't construct pyramids (well, other than a few Californians and the builders of the Luxor in Las Vegas). But like the ancient Egyptians, many of us try to look as young as possible, hiding our ages with artificial enhancements. Have enough plastic surgery and your frozen-in-place visage ends up looking more than a little like a mummy. Some even have their bodies frozen in hopes that some future scientist will be able to thaw them out and revive them. The Egyptians trusted in Osiris; the cold customers of cryonics trust in Science, and it's doubtful that either god is up to the task.

At the end of my visit to Egypt, I came face-to-face with death in two of its most memorable guises: in the gilded funeral mask of a boy king who never amounted to much in life and in the withered features of a pharaoh whose immense power and influence had long since deserted him.

Cairo's Egyptian Museum, the repository of priceless antiquities dating back thousands of years, held both. In the Tutankhamun galleries, I saw a work of art that I'd viewed many times in pictures: the exquisite mask that covered the face of the king who looms so much larger in death than he did in life. Formed from solid gold embedded with turquoise, lapis lazuli, and colored glass cloisonné work, it's topped by a vulture's head, a symbol of the pharaoh's power over Upper Egypt, and a cobra, symbolizing Lower Egypt. Its expression is tranquil and remote, gazing outward into eternity. I wondered what the treasures of a truly powerful king must have been, when even this minor ruler was honored with such splendor.

But in the end, it isn't this face that haunts my memories of Egypt, but that of another king: Ramesses II, whose mummified body is kept in a glass case in a room not far from the King Tutankhamun exhibit. A number of his fellow pharaohs surround him, all similarly desiccated and shriveled. Even the mightiest ones, the pharaohs who once ruled millions for long decades, look pitiful and small. To echo the wisdom of the Munchkins in *The Wizard of Oz*, these guys aren't merely dead: they're really most sincerely dead (perhaps it was a mistake to toss their brains away with the trash).

I was most fascinated by Ramesses II, who is traditionally associated with the pharaoh of the story of Exodus in the Bible. Though no direct evidence for this exists, historians do know that he lived to an extraordinary age—into his nineties—and that he had many wives and concubines and sired more than one hundred children. He built huge monuments and temples, and statues of him were erected throughout the kingdom, including the four sixty-five-foot colossi at the famed Abu Simbel Temple near Aswan. He was a military leader, a statesman, an emperor, and a god. And now he is a shriveled husk.

I thought of other faces of the dead I'd seen, usually at a visitation in a funeral home, not many centuries after their deaths. But no matter how long after their demise we view them, it's a remarkable thing to be in the presence of bodies whose animating force has departed (a turn of phrase that makes *dearly departed* ring true indeed). They're clearly human, and yet not human. Even the very ill, those who are immobile and barely breathing, are quantitatively different after they've died.

Perhaps the reason mummies fascinate us is that in viewing them, we get the chance to gaze upon death without the
emotion of grief. We can linger on the details simply with
curiosity: the matted, wispy hair, the skin draped like crepe
over bones, the teeth that jut out from between shriveled lips.
Despite the many centuries that separate us, our bond with
them is from one human to another. You were a pharaoh, I'm
a tourist passing through, and yet we're equal, somehow, in
this moment of connection.

But in the end, I think that mummification—and its modern equivalent, embalming—only emphasize the finality of
death. Both create a simulacrum of a person that's all the more
unsettling because while so much is similar, the essence is lost.
Seeing the mummies made me more determined than ever
to choose an alternative to keeping my body intact after my
death: burn me in a crematorium, wrap me in a sheet and bury
me in the back garden, put me on a platform for the vultures
to eat. Just don't try to stop the inevitable disintegration of the
flesh that once held my soul.

And instead of saying, "She looks so natural," I hope my
loved ones will say, "Boy, she wrung every bit of life out of that
body before she died, didn't she?"

At the Great Pyramid, as I stood looking upward in awe, a man
leading a camel approached me, his animal gazing at me with
the expression of disdain that its species has perfected.

"Ride?" asked the man. "I'll give you a good deal."

"No, thank you," I said, remembering my last jolting, pre-
carious ride perched atop a camel. I'd already had one overrated
travel experience that day and didn't intend to have another.
"But how about a picture?"

The shot is one of my favorite from Egypt: me grinning in
the bright sunlight, standing in front of a sneering camel, while
behind us loom the pyramids. I knew I was the equivalent of
a grain of sand to them, an ephemeral speck that would soon
be blown away by the wind. A minute before Herodotus had
stood there, and now it was my turn.

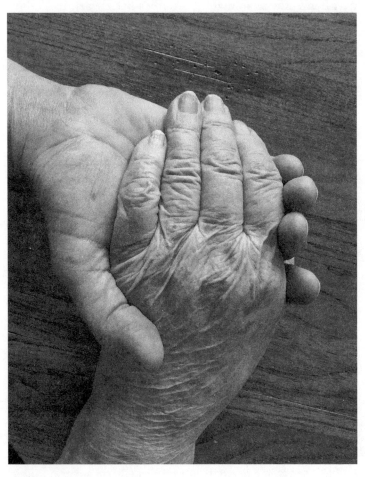

At the nursing home (PHOTO CREDIT: BOB SESSIONS)

2

God's Waiting Room

Nursing Homes

I'm talking on the phone with my sister, Julie, getting the update on her most recent visit with our mother. After I say good-bye to her, Bob comments on the fact that I'd laughed almost the entire way through the conversation.

Well, there were a lot of things to laugh at. My mother, for example, refers to her room at the nursing home as "upstairs," even though the entire building is on one level. She insists on having a Velcro-attached cloth draped in front of her room to keep out intruders, and at night she barricades herself inside by putting a table against the door—defenses that she's quite proud of, as if she's a medieval queen successfully defending the castle against invading armies.

These things could be simply sad, or we can find them amusing.

Despite her confusion, our mother seems happier now than she did during the years after she retired. Living on her own without the routine of work, she'd grown increasingly isolated and lonely, but she still refused to consider any sort of assisted-living situation that would have given her more social contact. When her doctor finally told her that she could no longer drive or live on her own, I think at some level she was relieved that the decision had been made for her. Now she's enmeshed in a community of people, even though she can't remember their names.

When I visit, she introduces me over and over again to the staff and other residents, sometimes several times within the space of the same visit. The aides give her hugs and say how much they appreciate her, and her face lights up with pleasure. She has a relationship with the other residents, too, but it's more distant, as most of them are even more limited in their social and intellectual abilities. One woman often follows us around the memory unit, shuffling behind us without saying anything, and I get a sense for why my mother needs the barrier at the entrance to her room.

One afternoon when I call her, she can only speak for a short period of time because she's playing a game that involves batting a balloon from person to person as they sit in chairs in the dining room. Her voice is excited. "I need to go—it's my turn," she says.

Later that day, I get the news that Mom had fallen out of her chair while reaching enthusiastically for a ball. She bruised her shoulder a little, the nurse says, but seems to be doing fine.

"You do realize, don't you, that this is likely the first sports-related injury in the Erickson family in several generations?" Bob asks me when I tell him the story.

It felt good to laugh at that comment, too, and to know that my mother is still capable of genuine pleasure, as limited as her life now is.

The five years that Bob's mother spent in a nursing home weren't relieved by much laughter. Alice's life in a sense ended with the death of her much-loved husband, Bill. During the fifteen years after he died suddenly of heart failure, her life became a shadow of what it had once been. Her dementia developed more slowly than my mother's did, seeping like a miasma through her consciousness over several years, gradually stealing her faculties and ability to care for herself. For years worry and anxiety plagued her, and once she moved into a nursing facility she missed her home terribly, not surprising for a woman who'd always taken great pride and pleasure in being a homemaker. Though the place was well run and comfortable, she often referred to it as a prison, a poignant comment for a woman who'd been a model of rectitude her entire life.

And then those complaints gradually ended, too, as almost all the parts that had once been Alice faded away. For a time she could still carry on a semblance of a conversation, stringing English words together with the right intonations but no coherence. Eventually all that was left of her was a nearly unrecognizable shell. By the time she died at the age of ninety-three, it had been a couple of years since she'd been able to have a conversation with her family. For her, the journey to death passed through fog and terrible disorientation—the equivalent, perhaps, of meeting the fearsome beasts that guarded the entrance to the Egyptian underworld.

To enter and exit the memory care wing where my mother lives, I have to punch a code into a keypad, a safety feature that ensures the residents won't wander the halls on their own. Doing so is always a reminder that I need to savor the times I have with her, as what lies ahead is going to be even harder.

A PASSPORT TO THE NURSING HOME

For many people, nursing homes are the last stop before the Final Exit. And a journey to them, as either a visitor or a resident, brings many opportunities for spiritual growth, if we could just get over being so depressed by them.

Though no one ever says, "When I'm old, I sure hope I end my days in a nursing home," an American over the age of sixty-five has about a one-in-four chance of spending time in one. Some stay for weeks or months, others for years. Too often they're merely warehouses for the elderly, a travesty of the word *home*. But care for seniors, thankfully, is changing—becoming less institutional, more humane, and more diverse.

Some facilities are integrated with day-care centers and foster child programs, for example, and others cater to particular interest groups and ethnicities, from retired musicians to Chinese American elders. Many have ditched the sterile long hallways of rooms and instead installed pods of living spaces clustered around a central kitchen and living room. Even the older-style facilities like the one where my mother lives can be remarkably good, with staff members who genuinely care for the residents and try to make the end of their lives as pleasant as possible.

It's easy to be sentimental about how wonderful it is to have multiple generations living under one roof, with grandma spending her last years lovingly tended by her children and grandchildren. But the day-to-day reality of this can be overwhelming for caregivers. In traditional societies, often grandchildren are assigned to care for those in advanced age, giving up their opportunities for a full life in the process. And in our society, many make do with a hodgepodge of care that stretches families—especially daughters—to their limit. To do what the nursing home staff provides for my mother, I'd have to quit my job and still hire additional help. Visiting her, I'm struck by how amazing it is to have these twenty-four-hour care facilities for the elderly.

Many of my friends are going through similar situations with their parents. Our conversations used to be dominated by talk about our children, their sports activities and academic pursuits. In the upwardly mobile milieu of my home city, there's peer pressure to have overachieving, impressive children, but no such social expectations exist in relation to parents. "They're making me crazy," says one friend over a glass of wine one evening. "It's never-ending. Just when we figure out how to deal with one crisis, another pops up. It's a geriatric game of whack-a-mole."

As the one-upsmanship of parenting morphs into the one-downsmanship of being a caregiver, we compete for the status of who has it worse with their aging relatives. We trade stories of doctor's appointments, insurance difficulties, and lost hearing aids. Worries about our children learning to drive are replaced by worries about our parents getting behind the wheel of a car.

These conversations have a comforting sense of solidarity, as the challenges we're facing are universal. And because death usually comes first to our parents, this process gives them one last chance to teach us some important life lessons.

The first lesson is usually about stuff: as in, we have too much crap, and our parents have even more of it. Their closets and shelves often overflow with books, clothes, knickknacks, mismatched dishes, photographs of people we don't know, games with missing pieces, and drawers full of plastic margarine tubs warped from the dishwasher, all of which we'll eventually have to exhume, examine, and put into piles for charity, the trash, or saving. That last pile is tiny, as what goes with someone to a nursing home is but a distillation of the essence of who they once were.

When we cleaned out my mother's house in a whirlwind of work, I had a series of profound insights. The first was that I don't need to save every rubber band that comes into my house, or keep magazines that I'm never going to read, or tuck away for safekeeping the packaging from every box I've ever received in the mail. I also realized that angels sometimes come in the form of the men who deliver industrial-sized dumpsters to the front driveway, and that if you're an in-law rather than a blood relative, it's usually best to keep your head down and your mouth shut (here's looking at you, Bob).

I saw, too, the ways in which possessions can become like a protective shell, a carapace built up gradually over many years. We have them so long and live with them so intimately that we think they're part of us—until we're faced with a crisis that makes us realize they were never ours at all.

As I carried boxes of stuff out of my mother's house, I thought of my sons eventually doing the same with my possessions. I wondered if they'd have a similar sense of disbelief at what I'd saved. "Just how many Virgin Mary statues does one person *need*?" I can imagine them saying to each other.

Once my mother entered the nursing home, her few remaining possessions arranged in her small room, I struggled to make sense of her new existence. This country to which she's immigrated has its own climate (almost always too hot for my comfort) and cuisine (try to avoid the tuna casserole, but the barbecued pork sandwiches aren't bad). I tried to call upon the same skills I use when I cross an international border: How do the natives relate to each other? What history has shaped this place? What are its unwritten rules?

In some ways the nursing home reminds me of a college dormitory, another age-segregated living situation where much of our personal autonomy is given over to someone else. Leaving behind the familiar environs of home, residents live in intimate connection with strangers, with most of the day-to-day details of their lives, from meals to entertainment options, arranged by others. Nursing home residents have something in common with hipsters moving into those trendy tiny homes, too, as people have to adjust to drastically limited living space. Radical downsizing removes the protective cocoon of possessions and sets both groups apart from the rest of society. Those in advanced old age, especially, enter a democracy of equals: as the end approaches, the divisions of educational levels, wealth, and social connections blur. My mother, who worked for decades in food service at the local college, moved into a room just down the hall from its former academic dean.

Visiting my mother, I'm also struck by how removed-from-time the place is. While calendars and clocks hang on the walls, and decorations shift from the flags of July 4 to the pumpkins of Halloween and then the green-and-red ribbons of Christmas, each day is like the next. Rarely venturing outside, the residents see the seasons pass at a distance, with winter, spring, summer, and fall experienced only through glass. My mother seems unconcerned about this and never expresses a desire to go outside, as if she's landed in a foreign country with an expired passport and knows she can never leave.

This limbo state is watched over by a being I've dubbed the Angel of Forgetfulness. Her actions are in some ways cruel, but at other times a blessing. My mother has lost so much—her ability to take care of her physical needs, to read, to carry on a conversation of any depth. But she's also forgotten the conversation in which my sister and I told her about her son's death. I give thanks that she's spared the grief of losing him.

The shifting relationship with our parents in the last stage of their lives usually involves a reversal of earlier patterns. For years we've looked to them for comfort, approval, and support. They likely held a large amount of emotional power over us, for good or ill. But now their personal autonomy is controlled by the staff members who happen to be working that day and by children who live elsewhere. Often for the first time, we get a full look at their finances and their health issues, their insecurities and anxieties. The emotional support is a one-way street.

I feel guilty when I admit that it's easier to relate to my mother now than it's been for many years. Living several hours away, I can't visit as often as I feel I should, but I'm paradoxically comforted by the fact that when I do visit, she'll soon forget that I was there. And when we're together, there's a tenderness that was lacking before. She isn't capable of wanting me to be different, and I know I need to appreciate who she is now, in this moment, because the fog of dementia is curling ever closer. We're both content with each other as we are.

There's little to talk about, but when we walk down the hallway we hold hands, something I haven't done with my mother since I was a child.

The next time I visited my adult sons, I found myself giving them instructions about what to do with me in my advanced age.

"When I get really old, don't feel you have to take care of me in your home," I told them. "I don't want you to sacrifice your own lives to take care of me."

Then I realized I hadn't nuanced my position enough. "But I'd like to live near you, maybe in one of those sweet little grandmother houses, so I can be close but not right in your face all the time," I said. "And I promise never to show up unannounced, either. But when I get too frail, you should put me in a place where someone else can take care of me. I changed your diapers but I don't want you to change mine."

They looked at me, their expressions reminiscent of wild animals caught in a trap. As young adults, the last thing they want to think about is having their incontinent, aged mother living in their backyard, shuffling onto the patio when they're entertaining. They started edging for the door.

As they left, I called out some final instructions. "Remember that I'll have a do-not-resuscitate order. Don't even think of putting me on a ventilator!"

THE BUDDHA IN THE HALLWAY

More than twenty-five hundred years ago, a young man had an encounter with an elderly person that changed the course of history.

Siddhartha Gautama was born into a life of wealth and privilege, the son of a king. His father, wishing to protect the young prince from knowing about the miseries of the world, raised him in a royal enclosure with no outside contact. But when Siddhartha was in his twenties, he decided to venture out on his own beyond the walls. For the first time in his life, he saw the ravages of age in the form of an old man. That sight—followed soon after by glimpses of a sick person and a dead body—triggered in him the desire to understand the sources of suffering. His father was, in a sense, right to protect him: encountering old age, sickness, and death can be rocket fuel for a spiritual crisis.

After years of wandering, pondering, and meditating, Siddhartha became the Buddha, "the awakened one." And ever since, Buddhists have recognized the importance of meditating on death. "Of all the footprints, that of the elephant is supreme," said the Buddha. "Similarly, of all mindfulness meditation, that on death is supreme."

This practice isn't unique to Buddhism, of course. When Roman generals led victory parades through the streets of

Rome, for example, slaves would be stationed behind them in their chariots to whisper in their ears, "Remember that you are mortal." During the Middle Ages, a less labor-intensive version of this was keeping a skull on one's desk, a practice common among philosophers, monks, and saints. Medieval artists often pictured the *Danse Macabre*, or Dance of Death, with a personified figure of death waltzing with both common-ers and kings. Puritan tombstones frequently bore images of a winged death's head or a skeleton with a scythe, sights meant to remind passersby of their own inevitable fates. And in Chris-tian churches to this day, the season of Lent begins with clergy putting a smudge of ash on the foreheads of parishioners as they intone, "Remember that you are dust, and to dust you will return."

But Buddhism, more than any other tradition, sees medita-tion on our Final Exit as a uniquely powerful form of spiri-tual practice. The Buddha summarized its precepts in the Five Remembrances, a set of teachings that's the spiritual equivalent of a stiff shot of whiskey:

> I am of the nature to grow old.
> There is no way to escape growing old.
>
> I am of the nature to have ill-health.
> There is no way to escape having ill-health.
>
> I am of the nature to die.
> There is no way to escape death.
>
> All that is dear to me and everyone I love are of the nature to change.
> There is no way to escape being separated from them.
>
> I inherit the results of my actions in body, speech, and mind.
> My actions are the ground on which I stand.

The modern world has done its best to run the other way from these insights. We no longer have charnel houses with stacks of bones (and honestly, I don't think it's a good idea to bring them back, despite the opportunity they give for spiritual reflection). Increasingly, funerals have a tidy container of ashes rather than a body on display in a casket. The dead bodies we do see are fake, the faux corpses in movies and on TV. And when we do encounter the real thing, it's often the body of a loved one, viewed in a time of overwhelming grief. The chance for a measured and philosophical appraisal of death—sitting with it, pondering it, and growing comfortable with it—is largely gone from our culture.

So maybe nursing facilities for the elderly are the closest many of us can get to this time-honored practice of confronting aging and death. If the Buddha accompanied me on a visit to my mother, I know he'd feel right at home. He'd be full of compassion for the residents with their halting gaits, blurred vision, and trembling hands, but he'd also likely poke me in the ribs with his elbow, prodding me to notice the abundant spiritual lessons all around us.

"How wonderful it is to be here!" he'd say as we walked down the hallway. "So many opportunities to learn." Then he'd sit down next to a resident in a wheelchair, gently take her hand, and invite her to notice how beautiful the view out the window is. In the memory care unit of my mother's Lutheran nursing home, the residents wouldn't be surprised at all to be chatting with a robed Buddhist monk.

I found another wise Buddhist guide that summer after my mother's decline and my brother's death: Kathleen Dowling Singh, whose book *The Grace in Aging: Awaken as You Grow Older* describes the ways in which the sufferings and indignities of growing older can be the catalyst for spiritual growth.

The trouble with aging, according to Singh, is that it sneaks up on us. While a terminal diagnosis frequently jolts people into contemplating spiritual questions, aging often happens so slowly that we can easily miss the chance to learn from it. Instead of blossoming, we collapse like a balloon with a slow leak.

Singh writes:

Although it becomes a little bit harder to do so each day, aging still permits us to evade the truth of our own impermanence in a way that dying does not. Such evasions obstruct awakening.

Aging simply does not have the gathered intensity of dying. That gathered intensity . . . is a crucible for transformation, for awakening. Simply aging, simply becoming an elderly person, offers no such transformative crucible. There is nothing in the process of simply getting older that, in and of itself, is going to make our eventual decline and illness and all of our losses either transformative or hopeful.

Whatever transformative experience we have of aging is dependent upon our own intention.

Lightening our attachment to self is the only thing that can get us through the losses of aging with some measure of equanimity and serenity. Singh writes of the transformative power of disciplines available to all of us, not just Buddhists: solitude, silence, forgiveness, humility, and opening the heart and mind through prayer and meditation. One of the reasons why our culture has a dearth of wise elders, she believes, is that so few take these paths. Instead we cling to status, unexamined habits of thinking and behavior, and a need to present a certain image to the world. Our world is full, alas, of elderly adolescents.

Singh's words resonated for me as I visited the nursing home during the first few months of my mother's tenure there. I realized that most of us simply become more comfortable in our ruts as we age. If we were judgmental and angry during our middle years, we'll likely carry those same patterns with us into advanced age. If our lives were centered on love, there's a good chance our final chapter will be illuminated by that emotion.

During her first months in the nursing home, my mother's main anxiety was money, which isn't surprising for a woman who lived on a modest income her entire life. She worried that she didn't have any cash in her purse. When I visited, she asked if we could go to the bank and then to the grocery store to buy

food. I explained, over and over again, that if she needed anything she could ask the staff. My mother-in-law, in contrast,
had other issues: her lifelong pride in keeping her house neat
and clean meant that she was perpetually dissatisfied in a place
where someone else was responsible for these tasks.

I look at their examples, and read Singh's words, and try to
take these lessons to heart. I know that my mother isn't capable
of philosophical ruminations at this point (and frankly, even
in her prime she wasn't much of a fan of them). But change
is possible for me. Instead of dreading my visits with her, I
try, often inadequately, to see them as times to honor her and
give thanks for the gifts she's given me, from my first breath
to a lifetime of love. I try to see the value of being forced to
confront my own mortality as I visit her. And when I leave the
nursing home, I breathe deeply of the fresh air, savoring how
remarkable it is to move without pain or difficulty, to get into
my car and drive wherever I wish.

These days, I don't need a skull on my desk to remind me
of the inevitable end of all life.

When we first visited the nursing home to make arrangements
for my mother's care, other memories filled my mind as soon as
I stepped inside its front door. Because my father had also lived
there before his death a dozen years before, I knew its arrangements of hallways and rooms, its smells of cleaning fluids and
cafeteria meals. Debilitated by diabetes and a series of strokes,
he faded away physically, but his mind remained much sharper
than my mom's until his final months. He lived for nine years
in this facility, one of the few men in a world populated almost
entirely by women.

When we spoke with staff members about my mother's
admission process, a number of them said they remembered my
father. He'd been a favorite of the nurses and aides, they said,
and they recalled that my mother visited him nearly every day.
Our conversation made me grateful, once again, for the kindness and interconnected web of relationships in my hometown.

After a few weeks in the regular part of the home, my mother was moved into its memory care unit. By coincidence, her room is the very same one where my dad once lived: out of nearly one hundred rooms, this was the one that happened to be open. She doesn't recognize it from the years when my father lived there, but my sister and I do. Snippets of memory surface at random, an interlayering of remembrances, from Christmases spent in the lounge area at the end of the hall to going for walks down the hallways with my dad in a wheelchair, my young sons at my side.

I'm glad I've had a break of more than a decade between these journeys to a nursing home, because the emotional price of the return trip is high. But I try to appreciate my good fortune in having had loving parents and a happy childhood. I give thanks for the excellent nursing home that took good care of my father and now shelters my mother. It could be much worse. I'm lucky, in fact. I repeat this as I punch in the key code to enter the memory unit. Maybe repetition will help me believe it.

"Your dad is with your mom a lot these days," a woman says to me.

I'm having an Angel Reading, a session with a friend of a friend who for sixty dollars tries to peek behind the veil between worlds. In signing up, I'd used the excuse of doing research for this book. "Surely I need to find out what the angels are thinking about this project," I told Bob.

Once I was sitting across from Allyson, however, all thoughts of research fled as she spent much of the time channeling messages from my father. He's proud of me, she said (all right, I realize this isn't likely to be wrong, given the nature of fathers). But there was other, more specific, information. My brother's happy and in a wonderful place, she said, as is my friend Mark, who committed suicide several years ago. She gave me details about their lives that I wondered how she possibly could have known.

I spent much of the reading in tears, especially at the messages from my father. Even before his death, it had been many years since he'd been healthy and vibrant. I'd forgotten what a good man he was. I'd forgotten how much I loved him.

At the end of the reading, Allyson told me that my dad is with my mom in the nursing home. "He's helping her," she said. "And when it's time for her to pass, he's going to be the first one to greet her on the other side."

When I visited my mother after that reading, I thought of Allyson's words. Of course I'd heard many stories of the dead giving messages to the living, but I'd never personally experienced such a phenomenon, despite my long-standing interest in death. I felt as if a new object had showed up on my spiritual radar, like a submarine surfacing from the depths, still vague in shape but growing closer.

Te Kaahu Ripo O Ngaa Rangi Tuitui from New Zealand
(PHOTO CREDIT: TIME UNLIMITED TOURS)

3

Joining the Ancestors

Among the Maori in New Zealand

For the Maori, the indigenous people of New Zealand, it would come as no surprise that my deceased father is keeping my mother company in her nursing home—and in addition, I might want to get a tattoo or two just to cement the connections between the three of us.

I learned about some of the Maori beliefs and customs relating to ancestors on a trip to New Zealand. As I toured, I had the usual reaction to the country: the hatching of a plan to try to immigrate. But in thinking back on this trip in relation to the Final Exit awaiting us all, what intrigues me most is how often ancestors popped up.

I'd traveled to New Zealand for a meeting of the Society of American Travel Writers. The adventure-travel writers went off to do bungee jumping and deep-sea diving, the foodies made a beeline for restaurants and culinary schools, and the movie aficionados went to *Lord of the Rings* sites with former orcs who now serve as tour guides (which gave me hope that pretty much anyone can be rehabilitated). As for me, I signed up for a weeklong cultural tour led by Maori who were eager to share their traditions with the larger world.

On the first day, I learned that the ancestors of the Maori came to a place they called Aotearoa, the Land of the Long White Cloud, at least eight centuries ago from East Polynesia, traveling in sturdy canoes known as *waka*. To this day, many Maori know not only their lineage stretching back many generations, but even the name of the *waka* that brought their ancestors to New Zealand. While similarities exist between their culture and that of other Polynesian groups, such as the Hawaiians and Samoans, New Zealand's isolation nurtured a distinctive identity.

Like indigenous peoples around the world, the Maori suffered greatly because of colonialism, discrimination, and oppression. They've had more than their fair share of social problems and poverty, as they struggle to find a way to reconcile their traditions with the modern world. But increasingly they're finding their voice and revitalizing their culture—so much so that they're now invited around the world to advise other native peoples about how they can follow their lead.

The Maori make up 15 percent of New Zealand's population, but they have an influence that belies their size. For generations, their culture and language were suppressed by *Pākehā* (New Zealanders of European descent), but within the past few decades dramatic changes have occurred. In 1987, Maori was made an official language of New Zealand, and most government agencies and many signs are now bilingual. The Maori won significant legal victories as well, including one that gave them a percentage of the lucrative commercial fisheries in the country. Laws were passed prohibiting the sale of Maori-owned land to nonnatives. Perhaps the single most important change is this: children can now go to school from kindergarten through college with all instruction in the Maori language.

The Maori reminded me of the Irish, another people for whom I have great affection. Both groups were long oppressed by powerful invaders. Both value stories, songs, clan, and family. And both provide a warm welcome to strangers.

Well, let me clarify that last statement. Technically, when the Maori meet people, they threaten to attack them.

This ceremony—called a *pōwhiri*—is an elaborate welcome ritual that dates back to the days when the island was divided among warring tribes that needed to prove their strength to strangers. It also explains why, when the English explorer Captain Cook first came to New Zealand in 1769, his men ended up shooting several warriors who meant no harm ("an honest mistake," a Maori man told me with a shrug).

The ritual typically begins with a challenge from one or more men, who make threatening gestures with spears and distort their faces into grimaces, shouting all the while. The lead warrior then drops a token, such as a leaf, in front of the visitors, and a representative of the visitors goes forward to pick it up, proving his courage by never breaking eye contact with the warrior as he does so.

And then the most magical thing happens. A female elder begins a call of welcome. We went through this ceremony a half-dozen times in New Zealand, and this moment never failed to bring tears to my eyes. The words were unfamiliar, but from the first time I heard them I recognized immediately what the woman was doing: she was weaving sacred space, making it safe for the two groups to meet. On and on she would chant, the unfamiliar cadences creating a place not only for the visitors, but also for their ancestors.

Next came speeches that alternated between the two sides. I was surprised that in most of the ceremonies we witnessed, women were prohibited from speaking after the call of welcome. The reason, we were told, is that women need to be protected. As life-bearers, they're more valuable than men and must not be exposed to any harmful forces that might be present when strangers approach. "You may think we discriminate against women," one guide told me, seeing my skeptical expression. "But keep in mind that a woman must start the ceremony. Unless her call of welcome creates the sacred space, nothing else can happen."

This ceremony concludes with the traditional greeting, in which each of the visitors presses noses with their hosts. It's a brief but intimate moment, meant to ensure that each person shares in the other person's breath. In doing so, their spirits, as well as their ancestors, are linked.

Let me count the ways in which all of this seemed strange to me. One: the mix of ritualized aggression and spirituality. Two: the length of the greetings, which took thirty minutes before we even got to the point of saying "hi." Three: touching noses with complete strangers. Four: sharing breaths. By the time I got to the fifth peculiarity, the part about linked ancestors, I was a stranger in a strange land indeed.

But when in Rome, do as the Romans do. And when you're in Aotearoa, get used to running into people's ancestors.

THE EAGLE'S MESSAGE

A man who wore his heart on his sleeve—or, more accurately, his skin—helped draw me deeper into the Maori story.

I first saw Te Kaahu Ripo O Ngaa Rangi Tuitui on a ferry that was taking our group of travel writers to an island near the city of Auckland. As we approached the shore, my eyes kept returning to the stocky, muscular man standing at the railing. Even among the hundreds of people on board, he was difficult to miss: every visible part of him was inked with intricate swirls and colored patterns, including his face and shaved head. If I'd seen him in a city, I would have crossed the street to avoid him. The tattoos were mesmerizing but intimidating.

I lost sight of the man as we exited the boat and walked a short distance to a beachside *marae*, a meetinghouse used for communal gatherings among the Maori. A marae is the heart of Maori society. The carvings that often adorn their exteriors and interiors tell stories and trace genealogies, while their interior is a place of *tapu* (sacredness). For the next twenty-four hours, the marae would be our base as we immersed ourselves in Maori culture and traditions.

"During your time here, we want the marae to become your home," our guide told us after we'd participated in the elaborate welcoming ceremony that by now was quite familiar to us. "This is meant to be a family experience, because once you are officially welcomed, you become part of us."

It did indeed feel like I'd joined a warm and nurturing clan, one with an insatiable appetite for activities. I went canoeing in the bay in a boat similar to those that first brought the Maori to New Zealand's shores, and wove flax leaves into baskets. I helped prepare the traditional *hāngī*, a meal cooked over hot stones buried in the earth, and learned the names of the children running in and around the building, though I never got clear exactly to whom they belonged. And at night, we all slept in sleeping bags on the floor of the marae, listening to traditional songs and stories as we fell asleep.

Through it all, we talked—about Maori families, religion, food, healing, ceremonies, art, and child rearing. And to my surprise, the man on the boat, the one with all the body markings, not only turned out to be one of our guides but also was a wise and gentle teacher.

Sitting together on a log overlooking the sparkling waters of the bay, I asked him about the patterns that swirled over his body and head. Te Kaahu told me that four years before, an eagle had visited him in the night, a bird so huge that it filled his entire bedroom.

"An eagle as big as a room?" I interjected.

He nodded. "The flapping of wings woke me up. And it came back five nights in a row."

It turns out that the eagle wasn't his first remarkable spiritual experience. At the age of twenty, Te Kaahu had received another vision, one that showed him the tattoos that would one day cover his head.

"I held out as long as I could," he said. "But after five nights of being visited by the eagle, I knew it was bringing me the message that it was time."

Te Kaahu had his face and head marked with complex designs, called *tā moko*. In doing so, he was following a long Maori tradition. Body art has been a valued part of that culture for many centuries. Because the head is considered to be the most sacred part of the body, to wear tattoos on the face is the ultimate statement of Maori identity.

As Te Kaahu told me his story, I became increasingly intrigued (as well as certain that I never wanted to be visited by an eagle the size of my bedroom). He explained the symbolism of his markings, saying that one arm told the story of his mother's lineage and the other that of his father, and that his facial tattoos were patterned after those of warriors of the past and symbolized the flow of the spirit from the sky to his mind and out through his mouth. He described his job teaching Maori culture in Auckland schools and how he mentors Maori adolescents in the criminal justice system.

"My markings tell the world that I'm proud to be Maori," Te Kaahu said. "I wear my ancestors on my skin. They're my guardian angels."

My time in the marae made me think of my own life through the lens of Maori beliefs. Their connection to nature was easy to understand (if you live in one of the most beautiful places on the planet, it's not surprising that you form deep bonds to it). The Maori call themselves *tangata whenua*, people of the land. Members of the various tribes distinguish themselves not only by the canoe that brought their ancestors to the island, but also by landmarks such as a river or a mountain to which they belong.

I'm a person of the land as well, I realize, though in my case it's Iowa. As a farmer's daughter, I grew up with its dirt between my toes, and as an adult I've relished exploring its lesser-traveled pathways. Flying back to Iowa after a long journey, I always feel a lightening of my spirit when I first see my home state far below the airplane window, especially during the growing season when its fields and waterways form a patchwork of green. Being among the Maori made me think of which landmarks I'd claim as my relatives—perhaps the trout stream that winds past the land my family once owned, or the bluffs that line the Mississippi River a few miles from where I grew up, or the wetlands that lie to the south of my home in

Iowa City. It doesn't seem like that great a leap to see them not only as home, but as kin.

The Maori concept of *mana* took more of a conceptual leap. I learned that mana is a person's spiritual power—their authority and presence. While it's similar in some ways to charisma, it goes much deeper. Unrelated to material success, it's handed down from ancestors as well as earned in this life. Mana is gained by living a moral life, particularly by caring for your family and clan. While people can acquire it during their lifetimes, they can also lose it by behaving unethically.

I recalled my friend Jackie, who radiated power even though she stood barely five feet tall, and my friend Lisa, who fills a room just by stepping inside its door. I could see how a lifetime of loving and nurturing people might have given them this sense of presence and strength. I thought, too, of people I know who have lost mana, including those who have wielded spiritual power for personal gain—a particularly dark path, no matter what faith you claim.

The idea of inheriting mana from ancestors was more of a stretch. It put an entirely new spin on my contemplation of mortality to sense that I could both receive mana from my forebears and pass it along to my children. I wondered if I needed a more conscious connection to my ancestors in order for this to happen. Perhaps that's why so many in the West are alienated and lonely: we're cut off not only from those around us, but also from the generations before us who could give us strength. In America, we might know our grandparents, or even great-grandparents, but the sense of being part of a chain of familial connections is largely foreign to us.

The Maori rules governing relations between men and women were another puzzle to me. I had a personal encounter with these rules when I approached a building near the island marae where pieces of wood were being carved. I couldn't enter it, I was told, because these were going to be installed on the walls and exterior of the meetinghouse. The spiritual energy of women is so strong that it could interfere with the sacredness of the process. Women were invited to see the carvings from the doorway but were not allowed to stand beside them. Only after the carvings were installed with the proper rituals would women be allowed to come near them.

I found myself torn between feeling offended and flattered (why, yes, I do exude powerful spiritual magnetism, thank you for noticing). I knew that this sort of division between the sexes can turn into plain old oppression and discrimination, as the popular Maori film *Whale Rider* dramatizes. But I don't think that the Maori I met were just paying lip service to the idea that women are more powerful than men. In fact, a guide told me that when European practices first filtered into Maori culture, women actually lost status, because their role in Western society was much more subservient. "I think the men were probably glad to have an excuse to put women in a lower place," he said.

I also knew that in New Zealand, I'd met many strong, vibrant Maori women—and the older they were, the more impressive they seemed. At one community meal, for example, I sat next to the man who was the male leader of the meeting-house. But after a while I noticed something curious: whenever the servers brought a new dish to the banquet, they first brought it to his wife for her approval. And during our conversation, she always took the lead.

Perhaps the best indication of female status came from a male traditional healer who told me about the long training he'd undergone. When I asked him if the regimen was the same for women, he shook his head. "Men have to be trained to do what women do naturally," he said, his voice matter-of-fact. "After all, they are more powerful."

ANCESTORS, LIVING STILL

For most of human history, ancestors have been venerated— and sometimes actually worshiped as well. I realized that in all my wanderings around the world, I'd missed this common form of spirituality that held intriguing implications for thinking about the Final Exit.

We do have some vestiges of a belief in the importance of honoring our ancestors. We make charitable gifts in someone's memory, for example, or name our children after deceased relatives. But in many cultures, the dead live on in much more significant ways. It's thought that they can serve as advisers, healers, and companions, helping their loved ones by sending subtle messages through dreams, seeming coincidences, or communications during waking hours that have the force of more than mere imagination. If we've lost our way, they can gently help us get back on our path. Some societies believe they can protect the material fortunes of a family, too, helping them in business dealings and guiding their decisions.

I already knew of the Mexican practice of feasting in graveyards during the Day of the Dead festivities, and that in China, many people have house shrines where their ancestors are honored year-round. More bizarre practices once flourished around the world, including eating the bodies of dead people to absorb their spiritual energy and periodically digging up graves to dance with corpses. And even today, members of the Torajan community on the Indonesian island of Sulawesi keep the bodies of loved ones in their homes for periods ranging from several weeks to several years. People treat them as if they're still alive by changing their clothes, praying with them, and giving them food (note to self: don't schedule a trip to Sulawesi).

Across cultures, there appears to be pretty widespread agreement that the dead lose interest in us after a couple of generations, perhaps because their spirits move on to other, more absorbing, activities. Ancestor worship isn't always benign, either. Some cultures believe that if you don't do the proper rituals, your relatives can cause trouble for you even from beyond the grave. This seems particularly unfair: it's bad enough to have problematic relatives in this life, without the prospect of them continuing to torment you after they die.

I was beginning to see that this whole ancestor thing was more complicated than I realized. At the same time, I envied the Maori, people who are embedded in a web of relationships that extend into both the past and the future. They can recite their ancestors going back hundreds of years and look forward to being honored by their descendants for generations. In contrast, most of the people I know can only hope that the Mormons will enter us into their genealogical computers somewhere in Salt Lake City.

When Christian missionaries first encountered cultures that practiced ancestor veneration, headaches ensued. One response was to reject the practice altogether, pointing to passages in the Bible that prohibit listening to the dead. But other clergy found a way to accommodate ancestor veneration by putting it in a Christian context, though it took some theological heavy lifting and a certain amount of shrugging of shoulders. They pointed out that in Christianity, particularly Catholicism, the saints can fill roles similar to ancestors. It's believed they can intercede for us on the other side, helping us if we pray to them. They're cheerleaders in our efforts to lead moral lives. And many churches, especially in Europe, have pieces of bone from long-dead saints, body parts said to have miraculous powers.

The more I thought about it, the more the Maori concept of ancestors didn't seem so strange after all.

My last two days in New Zealand were spent in the Bay of Islands region near the Waitangi Treaty Grounds, which preserves the site of the 1840 pact that ended hostilities between the Maori and Europeans and gave birth to the modern nation of New Zealand. Its elaborately carved marae, the most magnificent in the nation, sits on a hill overlooking the bay.

A tour near the treaty grounds gave me some final insights into Maori culture. We took a canoe ride with Hone Mihaka, a Maori chief who invites visitors to join him for a variety of interactive cultural experiences through his company. He first

tried to teach us how to paddle a canoe to the beat of traditional songs, a lesson that made me happy that I'd never have
to travel hundreds of miles across the Pacific with a group of
poorly coordinated and musically challenged travel writers.
Then he took us to a marae built in the style of a century ago,
a meetinghouse where he and his family seek to follow the old
ways while still living a modern life.

Hone introduced us to his twelve-year-old grandson, who
like his grandfather was dressed in traditional garb. Hone
explained that ten years ago, he asked his daughter if he and his
wife could raise their oldest grandson. His daughter was reluc-
tant, he said, but eventually agreed, because Maori culture has
a long tradition of grandparents being given the oldest grand-
child to raise. This ensures that at least one person in every
generation will be deeply knowledgeable about their traditions.

"Most of my people are too busy to listen to the old stories
and learn the old ways," Hone said. "That's why I asked to
raise my grandson, so that he can help carry our culture into
the future."

While I admired this practice in theory, I knew what my
reaction would've been if my parents had made a similar
request of me when my eldest son was born: no freakin' way.
It's easy to visit another culture and daydream about taking on
just the parts of it you admire. But this honoring of ancestors
is an entire package, and I know that I'm far too enmeshed in a
different worldview to ever fully enter into it. In my corner of
the world our ancestors stay dead and buried, thank you very
much. We may visit them on Memorial Day and leave flowers on their graves, but otherwise we wouldn't think of asking
them for advice or assistance.

But I could see that one advantage of this belief system is that
it could make death a little easier to bear—either your own or
someone else's. If you're simply one link in an unbroken chain
that stretches far into the past and extends into the future, an
individual death is set in a much broader context. The wisdom
of your grandparents will live on in your child, who becomes
one of the caretakers for an entire tradition. And your ancestors

are still intimately connected with you, as near as the air you breathe in the traditional touching-of-noses greeting.

Before leaving, I asked Hone a question: "Do you ever get messages from your ancestors?"

"Of course," he said.

"How can you tell if a message is from them?"

"Some things are *of* you, and some things come *through* you," he said. "The things that come through you are from the ancestors."

His answer made my head spin, but in a good way. I thought of my own ancestors, most of whom I didn't know other than as names on a family tree. What messages would they give me, those stern Lutheran farmers who lived a hardscrabble existence in Norway? Would they advise me on the best way to dry cod or tend goats? Share with me their rømmegrøt recipe? I speculated on what tattoos I could get to honor them. It might be nice to have some rosemaling, the decorative folk art of Norway, up my right arm. And maybe a Viking sword and longboat on the other, to honor the bloodthirsty branch of the family.

But maybe I was looking too far back, especially given the fact that my great-great-great-grandparents probably aren't that interested in me anymore. I thought of my paternal grandfather, in particular, who died when I was fourteen. When I was a child, he visited us several days each week on our farm, which had been his before my father took it over. I remember holding hands with him as we walked around the barnyard, a tall and lanky man in overalls listening patiently to my incessant chatter. My younger son, Carl, is named for him, a recognition of the influence he had on my early years.

My life is very different from that of my grandfather, but I would guess that the messages he'd give me—or perhaps does give me, if I could only hear them—are similar to those he gave me back then. He'd laugh at my jokes. He'd listen to my stories. He'd show me he loved me through his actions, not his words (because Norwegians probably don't change their personalities, even after death).

I've never received a message from this man who was such an important part of my childhood, but the year after our New Zealand trip, another travel experience brought him vividly to mind. Bob and I were visiting our son Carl, who was spending a semester studying at a university in Leuven, Belgium. One day we were walking home from the historic central square of the city, winding our way back to his dormitory through narrow streets on a misty, gray afternoon. At one point Carl, who was walking ahead of me, turned around to tell me something.

And I suddenly saw not my son Carl, but my grandfather Carl. There he was, looking at me through the eyes of my son. The impression lasted just for a moment, but it was so uncanny it made the hair stand up on my arms. It was more than just their physical similarities, I think—something more looked out at me from Carl's eyes.

I thought of the many differences between my grandfather, who'd spent all his years on an Iowa farm, and my son, who was already well traveled and worldly in his early twenties. But they were linked, somehow, and the distance between Iowa and Belgium, and 1965 and 2015, wasn't nearly as great as I'd thought.

Of all the stories I heard about ancestors in New Zealand, my favorite is one told to me at the island marae, the place where Te Kaahu had shared his vision of the eagle. A local man joined us for one of our meals, and afterward I talked to him about his life.

He said that he'd grown up in a Maori family but became alienated from his relatives as a young adult, losing his way because of alcohol and a long series of foolish behaviors and bad decisions. Eventually he realized how far he'd strayed from his cultural and family roots and resolved to mend his ways. He went to an elder in his community for guidance. He talked to him about his drinking, his depression, and all the ways his life had fallen apart. He said he felt worthless and alone.

The elder listened patiently to his tale of loss and heartache. When the man asked him what he should do, the elder sat for a long time, not saying anything. When he finally began to speak, he didn't address the young man's difficulties directly but instead told him a story.

The elder spoke of the young man's forefather, the one who traveled across the sea to New Zealand from Polynesia nearly a thousand years ago. He described how fearful the man was at the thought of leaving behind all that was familiar. The elder recounted how he stood on the beach looking at the ocean just before he set out in a canoe, and how he wondered if he'd survive the long sea journey and if so, what sort of life he'd be able to build in an unknown land. His mind was full of doubts about whether he should go, the elder said.

"And then he thought of something that made him realize it was worth the risk," he said, turning to the troubled young man before him. "He thought of you."

A grave marker in Rome's Protestant Cemetery
(PHOTO CREDIT: BOB SESSIONS)

4

Entering the Shadowlands

Hospice

Gray hair came early for me, but I didn't mind. I decided I wanted to look like the women in the photos of *AARP Magazine*, the ones with the stylishly cropped gray hair who are always doing something that elicits envy—catching a cable car in San Francisco, hiking through an alpine meadow, dining alfresco in the Tuscan countryside.

But skin is another thing. In my fifties I started to get little scaly patches on my face and hands. In my darker moments they remind me of decay on the underside of a fallen tree, the equivalent of mushrooms slowly eating away flesh. And gravity is beginning to catch up with other parts of my body too. These are not happy thoughts, because they inevitably lead me to a shocking conclusion: I am not immortal.

But of course, it's not as if it's a big secret that we're all going to die. It's just that for many of us, most of the time, it seems like an event that's going to happen to someone else, some hypothetical me far in the future. Spiritual teachers in many traditions spend a lot of time trying to get people to see the foolishness of this perspective. Along with funeral directors and casket makers, for them death is a growth industry.

"To contemplate dying each day calls forth an instant reordering of priorities," writes Kathleen Dowling Singh. "Just like a quick and deliberate shake of a kaleidoscope, it creates a whole new patterning, a whole new view."

I've seen that shake of the kaleidoscope happen many times in those who've received a terminal diagnosis. Even if they've managed to avoid any serious spiritual inquiry in the years leading up to that moment, death's imminent arrival often focuses their attention. Most are able to let go of the pettiness, the anxieties, and the prickliness that may have plagued them for decades. Lifelong jerks get a little less obnoxious. Introverts start opening up. Extroverts shut up so that other people can speak without interruption. Almost everyone I've known near death becomes a little nicer, knowing they're near the exit.

As a deacon I've long had an interest in working with the sick and have been trained in Healing Touch, a form of complementary healing. Because of that, I've often had the chance to be part of the last days of people, serving as a kind of midwife in reverse. Most of the deaths I've helped with have been from cancer, which slowly overwhelms a body cell by cell. But I've also been on the scene after sudden and unexpected deaths, from heart attacks to strokes and accidents.

To some people, the sight of a clergyperson entering a hospital room is synonymous with bad news. I recall a friend once recoiling when I visited him wearing a clerical collar.

"Good God, I'm not that sick!" he said. "Take it off. Right now."

I removed my ecclesiastical dog collar with pleasure, happy not to play the role of the Grim Reaper's Apprentice. But when I arrive at the hospital for a pastoral call, I sometimes wonder when it will be my turn to have a member of the clergy visit, and whether I'll be happy or sad to see them.

It's a shock to see a body after its life force has departed, no matter how the end occurs or how emotionally close you were to the deceased. The corpse is like a piece of clothing left crumpled on the bedroom floor, fundamentally different than when it was animated by the person wearing it.

I'm grateful to have made the acquaintance of death in a variety of forms, peculiar as that may sound. In a society where dying is so removed from most people's lives, we lose the chance to become familiar with its outlines and psychic shape. Familiarity can bring understanding, and maybe a little less fear of the inevitable.

These experiences have made me rethink how I want to go. I used to think I'd like to die quickly—crushed by a falling boulder on a mountain hike, for example, or hit by a bus crossing a street. But there's a lot to be said for knowing in advance you're going to die. You have time to tie up loose ends, say good-bye, and give thanks to God and loved ones. You can remove any embarrassing items from your dresser drawers, safety deposit box, or storage unit. And if your sins are weighing heavily on your shoulders, you have the chance to get them expunged from your spiritual rap sheet.

During my tenure as a writer of Iowa ghost stories, I found it curious how many of them involved a sudden death, one that left the deceased with unfinished business of some sort. I heard numerous stories of spirits coming back to tell relatives where money is hidden or to ask forgiveness, things they didn't have the chance to do in life. It's an argument for having at least a little advance notice of your imminent demise.

Years ago, I attended a talk given by a palliative care physician about this process of getting ready to die. He began by asking us to list on a piece of paper three sets of things. First, we wrote down five possessions that gave us pleasure; second, we listed five activities that gave us joy; and third, we named the five people we loved most in the world.

After we completed our lists, the doctor began talking about a hypothetical patient, a woman whose days were filled with the usual routines, joys, and stresses of ordinary life. But after she discovered a lump in her body, there came a cascade of medical interventions: first a biopsy, then surgery, radiation, and chemotherapy. After a year, it became clear that the treatments weren't working, and the oncologist told her that she should get her affairs in order. She entered hospice care, and gradually her world shrank to the size of her bedroom.

And throughout this story, the doctor periodically paused to ask us to cross an item off our list.

The possessions and activities went first, of course. Each was a choice—which would I hate to give up more, my laptop or my car? Biking or walking? Then it was time to start crossing off people, each decision an agonizing, *Sophie's Choice* dilemma. By now it was clear where this exercise was headed, and most of us, even the men, were borrowing tissues from the women who were organized enough to keep a packet in their purses. By the time the doctor's hypothetical patient died, all of us had gone through a similar shedding of what we held dearest, leaving us the emotional equivalent of limp noodles.

Buddhist teachers in particular seem to take great pleasure in pointing out people's inevitable deaths.

Well, not exactly *pleasure*, as my friend Scott explained to me when we met in a coffee shop after he returned from a weekend retreat during which he meditated on his own death. Yes, there are such workshops, and people are lining up to take them. "I only got in because someone else had to drop out," Scott said. I didn't ask why.

Not surprisingly, the weekend had been a powerful experience, beginning with a Friday evening presentation during which the leader (a Zen teacher of considerable reputation) had announced that everyone in the room would be dying on Sunday. She said they should select the form of their departure—heart attack, car accident, whatever—and then spend their weekend preparing mentally and spiritually for that event.

"We did a variety of activities, including writing letters to our loved ones and deciding who should get what among our possessions," Scott said. "Our teacher led us in a life review, too, where we looked back on significant events and turning points. And we spent a lot of time in contemplation, trying to get an experiential sense for what it meant to face death on Sunday. It was intense."

"Then why did you do it?" I asked.

Scott replied by describing his work as a therapist, which includes counseling people who are dying. He has always told his clients that if you avoid something important, you invest it with a tremendous amount of energy. "If you face it, if you let in what you fear, that energy dissipates," he said. "It doesn't go away completely, but it can become manageable. That's what happened to me during the weekend."

For Scott, as for most of us, we fear not only our own deaths but also the effect our leaving will have on those we love. "In many ways, that was the hardest part to contemplate," he said. "I had feelings of fear and immense sadness. But do I walk around getting pissed off because there's gravity? Death is the same sort of immutable law."

By the end of the weekend, he said, all that was left in him was love, compassion, and forgiveness. "I don't know how to explain it in any other way," he said. "I'm not a believer in the afterlife, but still . . . by the end of the weekend, something opened in me. It's all more of a mystery to me now, what happens after we die. But most of all I keep coming back to that profound feeling of love and compassion and forgiveness."

His eyes filled with tears, and we sat in silence for several moments, while all around us flowed the conversations and clatter of the coffee shop, the everyday details of life that too often obscure the truths hidden underneath.

This stripping of possessions, status, and relationships happens to everyone as they die. Even those of us who believe death is not the final end and that we'll get the chance to see our loved ones again can't deny that in the short term, there's plenty of sadness to go around.

Spiritual teachers of many stripes, showing the kind of irrational optimism that makes them both beloved and scorned, insist that this is exactly when things get really interesting. Kathleen Dowling Singh says that as we approach death, we undergo a powerful inner transformation. Even if during our lives we don't advance very far on a spiritual path, in the nearing-death experience we go through a series of spiritual stages, which include relaxation, withdrawal, radiance, silence, sacredness, transcendence, intensity, and perfection.

In case you don't have time to read her book, let me give you Singh's own summary of what's most important about the nearing-death experience: "Dying is safe," she writes. "You are safe. Your loved one is safe. . . . Dying, remarkably, is a process of natural enlightenment, of finally coming home to our true self."

In my own time spent in hospital rooms and at the bedsides of the dying, I've come to see the truth of her words. Especially for those with a chronic illness, death often comes as a welcome release from suffering and an anticipated next step on a journey to mystery.

But getting to that point can be a real bitch, because what most of us fear isn't death but the process leading up to it.

THE CONVERSATION NO ONE WANTS TO HAVE

Sometimes, the shortest journeys can be the most transformative.

Take, for example, what happened when Dr. Angelo Volandes started taking patients who had received a terminal diagnosis on a tour of the intensive care unit at his hospital. He wanted to give them a clearer sense for the kinds of procedures that are often done on people who are critically ill. As they passed by patient rooms, they observed people on ventilators. They saw the rush of activity when someone coded and how the medical staff worked furiously to get them stabilized.

Volandes led these journeys to the ICU to give his patients a realistic picture of what end-of-life care often involves in a modern medical center, which is very different from what's typically portrayed on TV or in films. After his patients toured the ICU, all of them prepared advance care directives that spelled out their wishes in case they couldn't communicate later. Not surprisingly, most of them chose not to include the extraordinary methods that may prolong life, but often at the cost of great suffering.

I was fortunate to meet Volandes when he visited my hometown at the invitation of a nonprofit organization called Honoring Your Wishes, which encourages advance care planning for everyone, not just those nearing death. I serve on the board of the organization, which has the difficult task of encouraging perfectly healthy people to think about their deaths—the equivalent of a *New Yorker* cartoon of the Grim Reaper showing up at a cocktail party, hovering over the canapés. We thought Volandes was a good person to spark a community-wide conversation about death, since he actually wrote a book on that very topic: *The Conversation: A Revolutionary Plan for End-of-Life Care.*

In his book, Volandes points out a distressing paradox in how most Americans die. The majority of us want to breathe our last at home, surrounded by those we love. Instead, two-thirds of Americans die in health care institutions, often after undergoing medical procedures that were performed because loved ones didn't know their advance wishes and doctors needed to protect themselves from potential liability.

"Americans receive some of the best health care money can buy; they also experience some of the worst deaths in the developed world," Volandes writes.

In his presentation, Volandes elaborated on those ICU visits that were so transformative for his patients. They turned out to be life-changing for him too. "We eventually had to stop doing them because hospital administrators got nervous about privacy issues," he said. "But I could see how people appreciated having more information about the medical options available to them. I started thinking about how we could make this information available to everyone and so we put together a series of videos that explain various end-of-life options. Seeing how well these have been received around the country makes me even more convinced that everyone should have conversations about their end-of-life wishes, both with their medical providers and with their loved ones. These conversations aren't easy, but they're vitally important."

I knew the truth of his words, having witnessed firsthand the contrast between people who died at home, kept comfortable by medical professionals but not subjected to harrowing treatments that cause pain and distress, and those whose death was marked by unnecessary suffering. And I was determined that Bob and I weren't going to be in the category of people who think they'll get around to doing this paperwork eventually but not now.

So we met with a facilitator trained in advance care planning, a motherly woman who led us in a discussion of the medical interventions we'd want if we weren't able to make our wishes known. We discussed these options with our sons, who will have legal authority to make decisions for us if we're both unlucky enough to end up in comas at the same time. We signed the forms, had them notarized, and then filed them in the appropriate places. I felt virtuous and well prepared.

Then I tried to do the same process with my mother.

At this time she was still living on her own and showed no signs of the dementia that would eventually cloud her mind. I had my little speech all prepared: I'd tell her about serving on the Honoring Your Wishes board, and Dr. Volandes's visit, and how Bob and I had done our paperwork, and how I thought it would be a good thing for her to do the paperwork, too, so we'd know exactly what her wishes were, should she not be able to communicate them.

I gave my presentation, using all my best techniques of storytelling, humor, and empathy. Still, my mother's face darkened. I talked faster, sounding increasingly like a door-to-door vacuum cleaner salesman who could see a purchase slipping away. I started throwing other things into the pot—ventilators, burial vs. cremation, hymns at her funeral, feeding tubes, cemetery plots, do-not-resuscitate orders. Everything was met with stony silence. I finally ran out of words.

Then came the blowback, because my mother, God bless her, was capable of quite an impressive head of emotional steam before she began her cognitive decline. And bringing up her death was the trigger for one of the worst arguments we'd had in years. She raised her voice, asking why I was so interested in having her die, and I felt my face get red as I struggled to keep from snapping at her. The temperature in the room dropped to arctic levels.

Eventually we retreated to opposite ends of the house.

"Well, that went pretty well, don't you think?" Bob offered.

Two months later, I got a phone call from my sister. "Mom signed the advance care papers when I visited this week," Julie said.

"How in the world did you get her to do it?" I asked.

"It was easy—when we met with her banker, he mentioned that she should take care of it."

"Did she argue with him?"

"Not a single word."

The somewhat tempestuous side of our relationship is a thing of the past now. When I visit my mother in the nursing home, it's a relief not to have things to argue about. Our conversations are nearly always pleasant: we talk about the weather, the food, and her work at the college.

"I'm slowing down some," she says as we walk down the hallway to her room. "But I don't want to go into a nursing home, so I don't mind working."

"You'll know when it's time to quit," I say.

We sit in the lounge together, admiring the view out the floor-to-ceiling windows. It's a cold winter day, but inside the building it's toasty warm. Watching snowflakes drift to the frozen ground outside, for once I don't mind the tropical temperature.

"It's nice here," she offers. "People are so friendly."

We talk some more about the weather, and the food, and her job at the college, and I give a silent prayer of thanks for the banker, who did what I couldn't do.

WHAT HAPPENS WHEN OUR EYES ARE CLOSED

While a terminal diagnosis can radically reorder our inner lives, there's another way to get a similar change of perspective: meditation, a spiritual neighborhood that for most of my life seemed like a gated community to which I didn't have a key.

It's not that I didn't try. But even with my good intentions and periodic resolutions that this-time-it's-going-to-be-different, I could never keep a practice going for more than a few days. It all sounded so good in theory, but when it actually came time to sit with my eyes closed, trying to clear my mind of thoughts, I instead thought about an endless stream of thoughts that needed to be thought about *right now*.

And then Andy came into my life.

Andy lives inside my smartphone. He has another existence as well, I realize, but for my purposes he lives inside that little handheld device, ready for me whenever I need him. His gentle guidance given through a humble phone app helped me during that sad year after my brother's death and mother's decline. The combination of the technology ("you've meditated for four days in a row—good job!") and my introspective mood finally gave me some commitment to the practice.

To my embarrassment, after a few months I became one of those people who keep bringing up meditation in conversation, extolling its benefits and urging other people to try it. This is more socially acceptable than being a born-again Christian, at least in my corner of the world, but born-again meditators can have a similar sense of evangelical zeal. I've discovered this amazing thing—don't you want to hear about it?

The problem was that the insights that seemed so significant when my eyes were closed didn't attract much interest from anyone else. "In my meditation this morning I was obsessing about something and then I had this great moment when *I just let it go*," I told Bob.

"And?" Bob asked. "What happened next?"

"I just let it go," I repeated, peeved that he didn't recognize what a breakthrough this was.

"Good for you," he replied, and then asked what else needed to be put on the grocery list.

Despite not getting adequate praise for my efforts, I was beginning to see the connections between sitting with my eyes closed and my efforts to come to terms with mortality. Perhaps in meditation, I could get a smidgeon of the peacefulness I'd seen many times on the faces of people approaching death.

While the French call orgasm *la petite mort*, a reference to the brief cessation of normal consciousness that occurs during sex, spiritual teachers identify a similar dying to self in meditation (though it's not nearly as much fun).

"When we enter meditation, it is like a 'mini-death,' at least from the perspective of the ego," writes Cynthia Bourgeault in *Centering Prayer and Inner Awakening*. "We let go of our self-talk, our interior dialogue, our fears, wants, needs, preferences, daydreams, and fantasies. These all become just 'thoughts' and we learn to let them go. . . . In this sense, meditation is a mini-rehearsal for the hour of our own death, in which the same thing will happen."

Bourgeault helped me see the connections between what I was learning from Andy (who'd spent years in Asia studying Tibetan Buddhism) and a form of Christian meditation known as centering prayer, which was developed in the 1970s by Thomas Keating, a Trappist monk. During an era when many people were turning to Eastern forms of meditation, he wanted to remind people that Christianity has its own set of contemplative practices. These techniques are deeply rooted in Scripture and have been practiced by many Christians over the centuries, from the desert fathers and mothers of the third and fourth centuries to sages who include Bernard of Clairvaux, Teresa of Avila, and Thomas Merton. Unfortunately, these practices gradually became confined almost exclusively to monastic communities. Monks and nuns learned them, but laypeople didn't. The centering prayer movement is trying to change that.

While I'd known about centering prayer for years, until my born-again experience with Andy-Who-Lives-In-My-Phone

I'd never pursued it seriously. But it didn't take much to shift Andy's instructions into centering-prayer terms. Instead of concentrating on my breath, I focused on my sacred phrase (everybody gets to pick their own, but you're supposed to choose something appropriately pious).

It was a relief, frankly, not to always have to talk to God in prayer. After more than fifty years, I'd plowed the same patch of ground countless times. He already knew my own particular set of neuroses and anxieties, so much so that I felt I could just number them instead of dragging the whole mess out again in another prayer: "Number five—you know the drill."

But in meditation, the goal is to get away from words. At first I tried to do an end run around this by reading a lot of books about meditation, all written by authors who use thousands of words to tell you that you don't need to use words. From them I learned about the differences between concentrative forms of meditation like mantras, in which you repeat the same word over and over, and surrender forms of meditation like centering prayer, in which you try to release your thoughts and only use the sacred word or phrase when your attention is wandering.

To be honest, I never got clear on the finely honed distinctions between different types of meditation. Sometimes I concentrated, sometimes I surrendered, but I knew the most important thing was to keep my butt on the cushion and my eyes closed. Voilà! I was meditating for the first time ever. I tried not to get cocky—all the meditation teachers warn against that—but I allowed myself a little bit of self-satisfaction, having finally managed to wade into the shallows of this time-honored spiritual practice.

I was beginning to see that I didn't have to meditate in a graveyard to contemplate death. All I had to do was close my eyes—because as I sat motionless, it became increasingly obvious that the only thing that separated me from nonexistence was the gentle in-and-out of my breathing.

The creature who met me each time I tried to meditate, however, was formidable: a hyperactive chimpanzee well-known in Buddhist circles as monkey mind. Every waking moment, that little imp is active inside our heads, swinging from one thought to another, capable of traveling across time and space with lightning speed, perpetually dissatisfied with the perfectly ripe banana, the here and now, that's right in front of him.

To help deal with his antics, I tried a variety of metaphors. I imagined myself rising above storm clouds to enjoy the clear sunshine of the blue sky above. I pictured myself as a pool of still water in the middle of a forest. I sat on a riverbank and watched as my thoughts floated by like boats on the current.

That last technique worked the best, but I was still chagrined by the sheer number and diversity of the watercraft passing by—worries, anxieties, thoughts about what I was going to have for lunch, memories of an article I'd read two weeks ago, plans for summer vacation, resentments about an incident in high school, philosophical musings about the mind-body duality, curiosity about how many people know what an Oxford comma is, and thoughts about needing to go the bathroom. All of it passed by each morning, a flotilla of the trivial and the important.

Sometimes I rode one of those boats for quite some time, and my meditation time was just an excuse for daydreaming. But sometimes—often enough that it kept me meditating—I experienced something else: Stillness with a capital S. There was a kind of weightlessness about this state, a clarity of heart and mind that almost shimmered. And more and more when Andy's soothing voice told me my session was over, I was surprised, as it felt like I'd been meditating for only a few minutes. It gave me a glimpse of what it would mean to have that internal, ceaseless dialogue turned off, or at least toned down.

I thought about the Buddha who occasionally visited my mom's nursing home, and how he never seemed upset when the tuna casserole was even blander than usual or when the fire alarm kept going off for no reason. I'd watch him sit in a corner of her room, his eyes closed, his breathing rhythmic, and envied the way he was able to seamlessly return to ordinary consciousness once his meditation was over. Sure, he was a figment of my imagination, but he still had the amazing ability to remain calm and tranquil no matter what happened.

And I remembered a friend who, shortly before she died, told me that she wished she'd taken more time just to *be* in her life. "I was always so busy," she said. "I felt guilty sitting in the backyard looking at the birds and the flowers. Now that's all I want to do, and I'm sorry that I have so little time left to do it."

> For those who want to save their life will lose it, and those who lose their life for my sake will find it. (Matt. 16:25)

This familiar but enigmatic claim of Jesus kept returning to me after I started meditating regularly. His words recorded in the Gospel of Matthew were followed by these questions: "For what will it profit them if they gain the whole world but forfeit their life? Or what will they give in return for their life?" (Matt. 16:26).

I was used to hearing this passage interpreted as a command to follow Jesus to martyrdom, or at least to volunteer at the downtown soup kitchen instead of binge-watching Netflix. But Cynthia Bourgeault gave me an intriguing connection between Jesus' statement and meditation: "There comes a moment when the ego is no longer able to hold us together, and our identity is cast to the mercy of Being itself," she writes. "This is the existential experience of 'losing one's life.'"

This interpretation of Jesus' words had definite advantages. When you meditate, your legs might fall asleep, and your back may ache, but it's much easier than being martyred, even if you're on one of those monthlong silent retreats where all the food is vegan and they serve herbal tea instead of coffee in the morning. It also helped me better understand a term used by Christian theologians in relation to Jesus: *kenōsis*, a Greek word meaning self-emptying. Jesus has always been held up as the exemplar of this process—in between all the healing and preaching, in the midst of the crowds clamoring for his attention and the authorities calling for his head, he clung to nothing except the love of God.

While I'd heard *kenōsis* recommended many times through the years, I'd never had much concrete instruction on how to do it. But as I read the Gospels again through the lens of Buddhist teachings about meditation, I noticed how often Jesus sought solitude in his life, retreating to pray in the wilderness, on the side of a mountain, or by the shore of the Sea of Galilee. He advised his followers to find a secret, private space of their own too. "And your Father who sees in secret will reward you," he promised them (Matt. 6:4).

And who knows? Perhaps he was counting his breaths during that time. Maybe he had found a way, sitting on a hillside in Galilee, to tame his monkey mind, and maybe this discipline was part of what enabled him to follow his remarkable spiritual path.

The more I thought about it, the more Jesus' promise of losing one's life to save it didn't seem all that different from what the Buddha taught. The Buddha spoke of inner awakening; Jesus preached about being born again in the spirit. Both encouraged me to build a bridge between my small self and something greater, truer, deeper—and both teachers said that the most important part of my practice happened not when I was on my meditation cushion or praying in secret, but after I opened my eyes and reentered the world in a new way.

And as I mourned the loss of my brother and faced the existential reality of the death that awaits us all, my sadness was often eased by this simple action: I sat on a cushion, I turned on a phone app, and I closed my eyes. On some days it felt as if I'd entered a Buddhist neighborhood, and at other times the kingdom of heaven.

The Mayan temple of Tikal in Guatemala (PHOTO CREDIT: BOB SESSIONS)

5

Descending the Nine Layers

With the Aztecs and the Mayans

In Mexico City, I turned a corner in a museum and there he was: the God of Death, a six-foot-tall, skeletal figure standing with clawed hands outstretched, his face twisted into a grimace. Mictlantecuhtli, the Aztec god of the underworld, clearly wasn't happy—and I wouldn't be happy either if my liver dangled outside my body, as his did. Standing before him, both repelled and fascinated, I recalled being at the Day of the Dead celebration in Chicago a few months before. Mictlantecuhtli had been there, too, I now realized, a shadowy presence behind the faces painted with the pallor of death.

I'd come to Mexico to learn more about the traditions that underlie Día de los Muertos, searching for insights from a culture that seems preternaturally comfortable with constant reminders of mortality. Even the shops at the Mexico City airport had Day of the Dead knickknacks, figurines that must add to the anxiety of those with a fear of flying. Skeletal figures wearing ball gowns and tuxedoes filled the shelves, looking like members of a raucous family who didn't want to end their partying just because they'd stopped breathing.

The first stop on my Mexican Death Tour was one of the world's great museums: the National Museum of Anthropology, which covers ten thousand years of Mesoamerican history. In its central courtyard, a huge column carved with intricate mythological and religious symbols supports an umbrella-like roof, while the surrounding buildings hold thousands of artifacts from the dozens of cultures and civilizations that have shaped the region. The color and drama of the history recounted in the museum made my own Scandinavian heritage look pale and repressed (while I take pride in my feisty Viking genes, most of my heritage, alas, has more in common with an Ingmar Bergman film).

The museum's exhibits showed how two cultures in particular have influenced modern Mexico: the Aztec (also known as the Mexica) and the Maya. Both groups had a somewhat *exuberant* relationship to death, to put it delicately. The Aztecs, who ruled central Mexico for two centuries before the arrival of the Spanish conquistadors in 1519, get the prize for sheer bloody awfulness. They loved going into battle, and even in their peaceful moments practiced a number of grisly forms of human sacrifice, typically of prisoners they'd captured from neighboring regions.

Much of their bad behavior can be blamed on the Aztec deities, who were a particularly difficult and hard-to-please lot. They demanded blood in exchange for pretty much everything, from keeping the land fertile to making it rain. To appease them, the most common form of killing was to cut out the hearts of victims while they were still alive, a procedure performed by priests at the top of tall, pyramid-shaped temples. Once the heart was extracted and placed on a ceremonial holder, the priests would toss the bodies down the steps (and if you're thinking this is as bad as religious rituals can get, let me break the news to you that cannibalism was the next step in the process). Priests and nobles also shed their own blood to honor the gods, using thorns to pierce their tongues, earlobes, and genitals, which I imagine significantly reduced the number of people wanting to become ordained.

While even an ordinary day in the Aztec Empire was likely to include a lot of death, if it was a special occasion, the temples literally ran with blood. For example, when the Templo Mayor, the major sacred site in the Aztec capital of Tenochtitlan, was rededicated in 1487, thousands of victims (the number ranges from four thousand to eighty thousand) were sacrificed over a four-day period. Even the conquistadors were sickened by the carnage—and grossing out a conquistador was no mean feat.

One of my reactions to learning about Aztec religious traditions, I must admit, was a feeling of gratitude. Any member of an established faith must sometimes apologize to the larger world for its crimes and excesses, of which every religion has quite a few. Christianity has the Crusades and the Inquisition, for example, and even the peace-loving Buddhists have an embarrassing parade of charlatan gurus. But just imagine you're an Aztec priest at a dinner party with visitors from out of town:

"And what do you do for a living?" they ask.

"Let's have dessert on the patio!" you say, because hardly anyone wants to hear details about your work when you're an Aztec priest.

At the museum, I learned that for the Aztecs, people's fate after death was decided not on the basis of how they lived, but rather on how they died. Most souls ended up in Mictlan, the nine-layer underworld, a dark, damp, and miserable place ruled over by Mictlantecuhtli, the god with the dangling liver, and his consort, the equally unattractive Mictlancihuatl, who had sagging breasts and a skirt made of serpents. The only good thing about being in Mictlan was that once a year you could return to the land of the living during August, when ceremonies honoring the dead included dancing, feasting, and dressing up in costumes.

Some people were fortunate enough to escape Mictlan entirely, including warriors who were killed in battle, women who died during childbirth, and captives who were sacrificed in a religious ritual (perhaps this belief made it a little easier for the prisoners as they walked up the steps of those temples). Instead, these lucky souls ended up in Tlalocan, a paradise of eternal spring.

The Aztecs, along with other Mesoamerican cultures, even incorporated death into their sporting events. Throughout the region, a game was played on an I-shaped court with sloping sides. The goal was to put a heavy ball through a ring, a difficult task since players could use only their hips, elbows, head, and knees to move the ball. The game was seen as a reenactment of the sacred mythology of the Aztecs, recalling the perpetual struggle between good and evil, light and darkness, and the god Quetzalcoatl and his rival brother Tezcatlipoca. And here's the quintessentially Aztec kicker: the losers were killed. Of course.

Say what you will about the Aztecs, they did face death with a certain joie de vivre. To them it was an essential part of the inherent duality of the universe: male and female, hot and cold, day and night. And life and death, the most significant duality of them all.

When Hernando Cortés led the final battle against the Aztecs in 1521, he and his soldiers were joined by more than 200,000 members of neighboring tribes. For many years the Aztecs had raided them for sacrificial victims; it was now payback time.

Once the Aztecs were defeated, Catholic missionaries began evangelizing. Their work was made easier by the fact that Christianity also had a sense for the sacredness of blood (though for Catholics, it was the blood of Jesus on the cross, as well as the wine-turned-to-blood of the Eucharist). It also helped that there were similarities between Jesus and the plumed serpent god Quetzalcoatl, both wise and kindly deities who were going to return to earth at some unspecified point in the future. The military might of the Spanish provided an additional incentive: convert or be killed.

Through the next centuries, the two traditions intertwined. Many of the Christian saints became linked with the gods of the indigenous peoples of Mexico. The rain god Tlaloc was worshiped in the form of John the Baptist, for example, another religious figure associated with water. And when a peasant named Juan Diego had a vision on a hill near a shrine dedicated to the Aztec goddess Tonantzin, the brown-skinned woman he saw became known as Our Lady of Guadalupe. The visitation confirmed that the Virgin Mary loved the native peoples of Mexico as much as the Spaniards.

Given all of this, it's not surprising that when the newly converted Aztecs wanted to honor their dead, their traditional August celebration was moved to the Christian holidays of All Saints' and All Souls' Days in November. Elements of these earlier rituals were incorporated into the Catholic holy days, including music, dancing, offerings of food to the dead, the ubiquitous images of skulls and skeletons, and also marigolds, which to this day continue to be known by their Aztec name, *cempasúchil*.

At the anthropology museum, a multimedia installation vividly conveyed a central truth of Mexican culture. A wall full of videos displayed people's faces, smiling and laughing, but as I stood watching them, they gradually were transformed into skulls, and then back to life again. The Mexicans know better than most of the world that even in the midst of vibrant life, death is always present, just beneath the surface.

AZTEC CREEPINESS

Today the remains of the Templo Mayor, the main religious center for the Aztecs, lie next to the country's largest cathedral. (In Mexico, as in many other places around the world, religious landmarks from different eras are often layered upon each other.) The sprawling archaeological site—a hodgepodge of stone walls, plazas, and ruins—covers several city blocks in the center of Mexico City.

The Templo Mayor was once the heart of Tenochtitlan, the Aztec capital. On top of its main pyramid were two temples, one to the god of rain and one to the god of war—the very spot that I knew had been dedicated with thousands of human sacrifices. It was hard to reconcile the peaceful scene before me with the carnage that had once taken place here.

As I ventured farther into the ruins, one place in particular fascinated me: the House of the Eagles, which was a sacred precinct for some of the most elite members of Aztec society. It was here that the statue of Mictlantecuhtli, the god of death that I encountered in the museum, had been found. A sign near the ruin described the rituals that had taken place here. Traces of blood are still detectible on the stones, it said, words that triggered a shiver of distaste in me. I pride myself on being able to appreciate religious expression in many forms, but the Aztecs stretched my tolerance to its limits. Just how much of a true believer do you have to be to extract a beating heart from a victim and hold it up to your god?

If much of contemporary society tries to ignore death altogether, the Aztecs had the opposite problem: for them, death was strangely, inexplicably seductive.

In a valley about thirty miles from Mexico City lies an even greater archaeological treasure: Teotihuacán. Begun in the first century BCE, this city reached its zenith around 500 CE, an eight-square-mile expanse of towering, multistepped pyramids surrounded by hundreds of palaces, residences, ceremonial plazas, and bureaucratic buildings. Home to as many as 200,000 people, it was one of the largest cities of the ancient world. And then, in the seventh century, it was abandoned, for reasons not entirely understood.

When the Aztecs arrived two centuries later, they were so astonished by the city's scale and grandeur that they concluded it must have been built by the gods. They dubbed the tallest pyramid the Temple of the Sun and the next in size the Temple of the Moon, believing that the two major celestial bodies had been created there. And with their usual predilection for connecting everything they found to death, the two landmarks were linked by a road they called the Avenue of the Dead, the name it bears to this day.

I knew what those first Aztec visitors must have felt when they entered Teotihuacán, because I experienced it too: a sense of unreality and awe. Walking the expansive Avenue of the Dead, I first passed by the Temple of the Sun, which towered more than two hundred feet above me. A short distance away, the Temple of the Moon was just slightly smaller. In between were the remains of hundreds of buildings, giving a sense for the bustling life that once filled this metropolis. The scale and grandeur of the enormous site made me recall being at Luxor and Giza in Egypt—the only other places I've been that can at all compare.

Pointing at the Temple of the Moon, our guide showed us how its shape mimics that of the mountain behind it. "The temples were built because the priests didn't have time to climb a mountain each day," he said. "Instead they went up the steps of the temple to reach a high place where they could communicate with their gods."

I thought of the mountains climbed by religious figures in my own tradition, from Moses on Mount Sinai to Jesus on Mount Tabor. The urge to go *up* to talk to God seems to be perennial and cross-cultural. I'd felt it myself, more than a time or two.

My musings were interrupted by a loud, roaring sound that made me jump.

"That's a jaguar," explained the guide. Seeing my startled look, he added, "The sound is made by a whistle sold by the vendors here. The jaguar was one of the animals most highly prized by the ancient peoples of Mexico."

That wild, piercing sound is indelibly linked to my memories of Teotihuacán, a symbol of the enigmatic power of its massive structures. If the Aztecs were an inexplicable culture to me, the people who constructed this city were even more of a mystery. I felt like an ant as I wandered through what they'd built, the pyramids so far above me that I could barely see their tops.

Trying to convince myself I wasn't nearly as scared of heights as I thought, I climbed the steep and narrow steps of the Temple of the Moon, clutching a flimsy guide rope that didn't seem nearly strong enough to prevent a fall. At the top, I gazed at the expanse of Teotihuacán spread below me, baking in the hot Mexican sun. I wondered what rituals had taken place on this very spot and scoured the stones beneath my feet for telltale stains of blood, but I saw nothing.

After descending the steps—a process even scarier than coming up—I followed our guide to another incredible structure: the Temple of the Feathered Serpent, which lies at the other end of the Avenue of the Dead. Like many temples in Mesoamerica, it contains within it a series of smaller structures, because the native peoples of this region often built over existing buildings to create even larger and more impressive edifices. Archaeologists have removed the outer layer of this temple, cracking it open like an egg to reveal an inner pyramid with a remarkable facade. A series of finely carved heads jut out from its lower level. The gargoyle-like figures alternate between Quetzalcoatl, the feathered serpent god, and Tlaloc, the god of rain. The heads had once been brightly painted, a fact I recalled from seeing a replica of this temple in the National Museum of Anthropology, but even in their current brown, weathered state they were striking.

"The period between when this pyramid was completed and when it was covered up by another layer was probably only around thirteen years," our guide said. "But those who lived here likely knew that these heads were underneath, like the skeleton inside a body."

As he spoke, I thought of the videos in the museum, the constant shift of perspective between what is on the surface and what lies underneath.

At the end of our tour, we returned to the Temple of the Sun, an appropriate place to hear about the final days of the civilization that had built Teotihuacán. Our guide explained that around the year 600 CE, invading armies had conquered the people who lived here. Its citizens scattered, leaving the city to their enemies.

"But the group that attacked Teotihuacán didn't stay very long," the guide said. "The mystery is why its original residents didn't return to the city they'd worked so long and hard to build. Perhaps it was because they believed so strongly in the duality of life and death. The city was born, it flourished, and it died. And then its time was done."

In the distance I could hear the sound of a jaguar whistle, played by a vendor trying to entice a tourist into buying an inexpensive souvenir. But for a few moments, the sound seemed to come from much farther away—not in distance, but in time.

LEARNING FROM THE MAYANS

Still pondering what I'd learned from our stay in Mexico City, I next headed south to make the acquaintance of the Maya, another culture that has profoundly shaped Mexico. I was curious to learn what the Mayans could teach me about mortality and death—and more than a little happy to leave the Aztecs behind.

Flourishing between the third and ninth centuries in cities located deep in the jungles of Central America, the Mayans were master mathematicians and astronomers who mapped the movements of the stars and planets with great accuracy. They developed complex writing and mathematical notation systems and had multiple calendars geared to various celestial phenomena. The New Age fuss in 2012, when some predicted that the world was going to end, was related to the completion of a 5,125-year Mayan calendar cycle.

Bob and I had signed up for a tour called Maya Temples of Transformation, a weeklong adventure offered by a company specializing in spiritually oriented journeys around the world. I knew we were in for an interesting trip when on our ride from the airport to the hotel, a couple of our fellow tour members had an extended conversation about their personal interactions with archangels. Bob looked at me with a raised eyebrow. I shrugged my shoulders. While I was enthusiastic about the trip, he'd been more skeptical, an occupational hazard of having a PhD in philosophy.

But the description of the tour had intrigued us both. Instead of seeing the Mayan sites from a solely historical perspective, the tour was designed to be experiential, introducing us to contemporary forms of Mayan spirituality as we explored three major archaeological sites that were once capitals of powerful city-states: Palenque and Yaxchilan in Mexico and Tikal in Guatemala.

That evening we met the rest of our dozen comrades, who hailed from Australia, Canada, and England as well as the United States. While their ordinary lives were filled with the mortgages, jobs, and other accoutrements of middle-class life, on vacation they sought out spiritual mysteries in exotic locales. "I've visited pyramids all over the world," one man told me. "I've been to Egypt once and Machu Picchu twice and three times to Mayan sites in Mexico."

As the evening went on, I fought a growing sense of disorientation. Usually I'm the designated spiritual person in any group, the one who has all the surrounding holy sites on her radar and is most likely to throw around references to energy. But in this crowd, I was a rank amateur. I listened with a green flicker of envy as a woman told a story of being in one of the Great Pyramids at Giza. Instead of feeling claustrophobic and germ conscious in the pharaoh's burial chamber, as I'd been, she'd been swept up in a vision that included rocketing up to the heavens and then growing in size until she was the same height as the pyramid.

When she heard I'd been in that very chamber, she asked what I'd experienced.

"It was very . . . interesting," I said weakly. "I'm not sure I can even describe it."

She nodded. "I know. The power there is overwhelming. It's beyond words."

My dilemma grew as the week went on. At each of the Mayan sites, many of my fellow travelers had remarkable experiences. We'd be standing together in front of a temple, gazing upward, when suddenly they'd get a flood of past-life memories that had happened at that very spot. Meanwhile, I'd be thinking about whether I should reapply sunscreen. At dinner one night, a woman told me that the Egyptian god Thoth had sent her a message earlier in the day. And one afternoon a woman started using words I didn't understand, and then explained to me that she was speaking Galactic, a language she'd received from space several years before.

Bob was having his own issues. At dinner on the second evening of our tour, he got into a metaphysical tussle with another group member over the lost continent of Atlantis and the Akashic Records (which are said to hold a description of all human events, thoughts, and emotions). Bob persisted in arguing against the existence of either, despite my repeated kicks under the table and the pitying looks of our companions, who were clearly wondering how a seemingly well-educated person could have such big gaps in his knowledge.

Back in our room that night, we had our first—and I hope our last—argument over the existence of Atlantis.

"It's a harmless belief," I said. "And besides, no one wants a philosophical lecture on their vacation."

"Philosophers do."

"We're not traveling with philosophers."

We went to bed in stony silence.

The next morning, however, our tempers had cooled. Bob pledged to keep his mouth shut, even if people were violating his understanding of the laws of rationality, and I reassured him that he could believe anything he wanted privately, as long as he didn't lecture people about it in public.

But a funny thing happened to us as the week went on: we got into the spirit of the trip. The New Age vibe started to feel, well, perfectly comfortable. For one thing, our fellow tour members were so good-hearted and friendly, despite their unusual beliefs. It helped, too, that those who were having incredible spiritual experiences weren't lording them over us.

"It's actually a bit of a burden getting past-life information at unexpected times," one of them told me. "It can make it hard to concentrate on my job in a real estate office."

We were warmed, too, by the kindness of our tour leaders, especially Miguel, a Mexican shaman who had studied with Mayan spiritual teachers for decades and whose unassuming manner masked deep wisdom. At each of the sites he led us in ceremonies, inviting us to enter into the spirit of the place with our hearts, not just our minds.

My conversations with Miguel elicited my own philosophical conundrum. According to him, the Mayans did not practice human sacrifice, or at least not very frequently—an assertion that contradicted what I'd learned about Mayan history from my own studies as well as the exhibits at the anthropology museum in Mexico City. When I quizzed him about the discrepancy, he didn't seem overly concerned with the historical record.

"The Mayans knew that a spiritual seeker's ego has to undergo a symbolic death in order to be reborn," he explained. "The problem with the Aztecs is that they took these mystical truths literally, but the Mayans always understood them as metaphors."

As the week went on, I found myself caring less about historical accuracy myself. Even if the ancient Mayans did practice human sacrifice, their descendants today don't follow their example, and the magnificent temples they built can still be holy sites for contemporary seekers.

I was reminded, too, of studies I'd read about how psychologically healthy people often rewrite their past. They don't forget the tragedies and hard times of their earlier years, but with the perspective of age they often recast them into something less problematic. Perhaps cultures can do a similar thing. Miguel may have been liberally reinterpreting parts of Mayan history, but it was in the service of a good cause. He was keeping the parts of his tradition that are useful and meaningful. We don't need human sacrifice, so he left it behind.

Of the three Mayan sites we visited, Yaxchilan—the smallest—was my favorite. This was partly because of the Indiana Jones style in which we traveled to it: a forty-five-minute boat ride on the Usumacinta River on the border between Mexico and Guatemala. Along the way we passed mile after mile of dense rain forest with occasional crocodiles sunning themselves on the riverbanks. At the end of our voyage, we hiked up a steep hill and then walked down a winding forest path until we finally arrived at the archaeological site.

Miguel explained that Yaxchilan had been the capital of a jungle kingdom that reached its height during the reigns of Lord Shield Jaguar and his son Bird Jaguar, two Mayan leaders of the eighth century who made me wish contemporary politicians had animal names. More than 120 structures were built here, though only a small number of them have been excavated.

As we approached the entrance to Yaxchilan, Miguel gathered our group into a circle and filled our cupped hands with a small amount of scented water. As we splashed the water over our heads, I recognized a classic rite of purification, a common feature of nearly all religions. Next Miguel gave us a few drops of an aromatic oil that we used to anoint our foreheads—again, something I was familiar with in my own Christian tradition.

Miguel then directed us to put out our hands once again. "We will make an offering to the spirits of this place as we enter their home," he said, going around the circle to pour a small mound of corn kernels into our hands. "As you walk into Yaxchilan, you can honor them by throwing the kernels along the path."

Then we filed, one by one, into a shadowed passageway of stone, which wound around in the darkness for about fifty feet before we climbed a small flight of steps. As we ascended, I could see the brilliant green of the jungle framed by a doorway ahead of us. The transition from darkness into light felt mythic and ancient.

At last we emerged into the full expanse of Yaxchilan. With each step we took, the sounds of the forest became louder:

the shrill caws and melodic twittering of birds and the rasp of insects. The greenery pressed close to the buildings, as if it was eager to overtake them once again.

After passing by several sets of low-lying ruins, we saw a temple on a hill above us, a landmark reached by a set of narrow, steep steps.

"Before we climb up to the temple, let us gather together for a ceremony," Miguel said.

We formed a circle around him and watched as he took out the elements of the ritual—small wooden bowls that he filled with water, as well as a drum, incense, and pieces of brightly patterned cloth. He invited us to place our own sacred offerings in the center of the circle, and people came forward with stones, crystals, and other symbolic items.

I looked around the circle at my fellow travelers, all dressed in the white clothing that Miguel had suggested we wear that day. I could see how seriously they were taking this ritual. I was struck, too, by the silence that had fallen upon us—a hint that the holy was approaching.

And then, as if on cue, howler monkeys in the trees above us began a chorus. The guttural, loud sounds were unlike anything I'd heard before—the essence of the jungle, distilled in sound.

Those monkeys continued to serenade us during the ceremony, which Miguel led with graceful dignity. After lighting some pieces of incense in a bowl, he walked around the circle, stopping before each of us so that the scented smoke could briefly envelop us. Next he picked up a drum and began to chant, his voice rising and falling in unfamiliar cadences. When he nodded at us to join him, we took up the chorus, echoing the simple, repetitive phrases. For quite some time we chanted, the song rising in volume, and then declining, so that the sounds of the monkeys could be heard again. Miguel stood silent and motionless, his eyes closed, his expression serene. The energy slowly dissipated, seeping back into the earth from which it seemingly had sprung.

For the rest of the afternoon, as I wandered amid the ruins of Yaxchilan, the ceremony led by Miguel framed my experience. It gave me a glimpse of why the Mayans chose to build temples here in the midst of the forest, places where the spirits of the earth could be honored.

At the end of our visit, as we walked through the jungle on our way back to the boat, I complimented Miguel on the beauty of the ceremony he'd led.

"The most important part of a ceremony is the love in your heart," he replied. "If you don't have that, it doesn't make any difference what rituals you do. And if you have that love, all the rituals will work, no matter how you do them."

The archaeological site of Palenque offered additional grist for thinking about the Final Exit, in part because of a remarkable discovery made by Alberto Ruz Lhuillier in 1952. In what would be hailed as the New World equivalent of the opening of King Tut's tomb in Egypt, Lhuillier found the tomb of Pakal, who ruled Palenque for nearly seventy years in the seventh century. Under Pakal's leadership, the settlement grew from obscurity into a powerful city, with impressive monuments and temples lining its avenues, including the building that would eventually become his tomb.

I'd seen some of the contents of Pakal's burial chamber in the National Museum of Anthropology, including the striking jade mask and elaborate jewelry he'd worn for his journey to the underworld. This finery had transfixed me for quite some time, both because of the beauty of its craftsmanship and because of its sheer weirdness. For one thing, Pakal entered eternity wearing the world's largest earrings, with long spokes that jutted outward for almost a foot. And his burial mask had crossed eyes, which were considered beautiful in Mayan culture. (Here's a chilling little historical tidbit: Mayan parents hung balls in front of their babies' eyes to encourage this tendency.)

But the most intriguing part of Pakal's treasure was the massive lid of his sarcophagus, a twelve-by-seven-foot slab of limestone carved with a complex design that people have been trying to figure out ever since it was discovered. The image shows a man either descending or ascending a World Tree, a mythological symbol that has roots in the under-world, a trunk in this world, and its branches in paradise. The man wears the beaded skirt associated with the Mayan maize god, and surrounding him is a protective boundary of sacred symbols.

In the 1960s, Erich von Däniken thought he'd figured out the secret encoded in this design. In his book *Chariots of the Gods*, he posited that the man is likely an ancient astronaut in a rocket ship, a thesis that's been known to make reputable anthropologists put their heads in their hands and groan.

When I asked Miguel about the ancient-aliens hypothesis, he smiled. "There's no need to involve astronauts," he said. "The symbols are all about spiritual transformation, which the Mayans had been studying for centuries."

Once we reached the archaeological site, our first stop was the place where Pakal is entombed, a building called the Temple of the Inscriptions. This beautifully proportioned pyramid of weathered limestone has nine sets of steps that echo the nine layers of the underworld. It's named for the hundreds of glyphs (the Mayan form of writing) that adorn the inner walls of the building at its top, the temple where ceremonies were once held. Miguel explained that the pyramid was originally painted red, with its carvings detailed in bright colors. But even in its present form, it's an exquisite building, a splendid home in which to spend eternity.

Looking at it, I thought of the many rulers throughout history who shared the impulse to build something grand to house their earthly remains. I felt a sense of gratitude for their narcissism, because these monuments display the splendor of their cultures in permanent form. And I thought of the jade mask that had covered the face of Pakal, hiding mortal flesh that gradually dissolved into bone, despite the grandeur of the temple above him.

At dinner that evening, we talked about our impressions of Palenque.

"That stuff about ancient aliens is pretty ridiculous, isn't it?" asked a woman, the same person who'd argued with Bob about the existence of the lost continent of Atlantis. "The Mayans didn't need any help to create the wonders of their civilization."

I glanced at the woman who spoke Galactic, wondering if this would set her off, but she was part of another conversation and hadn't heard the comment. Then, seizing the opportunity to serve as the Grim Reaper's press agent, I introduced the topic of death, asking the people sitting around me what they thought happened after we breathed our last.

The discussion that followed made me realize that I'd never been in a group of people who seemed less concerned about their own mortality. They were all absolutely certain that they'd had many past lives and that after their current life ended, they'd get the chance to come around again.

"The body is just a shell, and when we die it drops away," one person said. "Then we get the chance to pick our next incarnation, choosing exactly what we want to experience in our next life."

Even though on many days I believe some variation of this myself, their certainty was a little unsettling. Part of it was their seeming trivialization of the sorrows that shadow human existence. If we all choose our incarnations, the tragedies that happen to us can just be chalked up to what we'd agreed to before birth. I could perhaps accept this philosophy in relation to my own life, for honestly, it's been a good ride. But applying it to other people's lives made me pause. What about those who live in abject poverty, or who suffer from terrible diseases, or who are brutalized by violence and war? Did they choose their incarnations, and if so, what in the hell were they thinking?

In the end, a philosophy that doesn't fully acknowledge the pain of suffering and death doesn't make sense to me, no matter how appealing it might be at first acquaintance.

I resonated more with these words from Miguel: "When we die, we owe Mother Earth our body in return for all we've taken from her during our lives," he said. "But our spirit lives on."

The most thoughtful response of all came from the owner of the tour company, Helen. When I asked her about death, a look of sadness crossed her face. She told me of the recent death by drowning of a young man who was dating her teenage daughter, a loss that had grieved an entire community. That experience deeply changed her, she said.

"I think the death of a loved one, especially someone who dies unexpectedly and prematurely, can be an initiation," she concluded. "The outpouring of grief for that young man was one of the most remarkable things I've ever experienced. It changed me. It changed all of us."

Back in Iowa, I ruminated about my time among the Aztecs and Mayans. As much as I searched my subconscious, I couldn't find any glimmers of past-life memories, with them or any other group. And my time spent with our New Age friends had shaken some of my assurance about what I actually believed about the afterlife. I wondered how many times my own theorizing about what happens to us after death had seemed glib to those whose lives were shadowed by loss.

I kept thinking back, too, to the Day of the Dead celebration I'd attended in Chicago. While I could now see more clearly its ties to pre-Christian traditions, I also appreciated how the modern Mexicans have escaped the Aztec vortex. Despite the ubiquitous skeleton figurines for sale in Mexico, most people there seem to treat death with an appropriate mixture of respect and dismissal. They don't focus on it to the detriment of everything else (an impulse that's all too seductive, for both individuals and entire cultures). Instead they welcome dead loved ones back and then tell them to leave again.

And those Aztecs . . . well, what had I learned from them, other than how to turn religion into a horrible bloodbath? Perhaps this: I thought of people I knew who'd had their hearts symbolically torn open from overwhelming tragedies. Maybe there's a sliver of truth in the Aztec belief that such people have a special paradise awaiting them, a compensation for the sorrow that haunts their lives in this world.

On my desk I placed a smiling, brightly painted skull I'd purchased from a shop in the Mexico City airport. Each day as I work, its hollow eyes, ringed by flowers, remind me of what awaits us all.

An angel in Rome's Protestant Cemetery (PHOTO CREDIT: BOB SESSIONS)

6

Crossing the Jordan

Funerals

"Sometime around 1830, people stopped dying and started falling asleep."

Loren Horton, the retired state historian of Iowa, seemed abnormally cheery for someone who has spent much of his career studying death—in particular, the funeral customs of the Victorian era from 1837 to 1901. Over coffee he gave me a primer in how nineteenth-century Brits and Americans dealt with mortality, his dry sense of humor making the subject so entertaining that I wondered if he'd ever considered doing stand-up comedy at funeral directors' conventions.

While people in the eighteenth century tended to be relatively stoic and fatalistic in their approach to death (think of those Puritan tombstones bearing skulls and crossbones), in the nineteenth century death got a makeover. Customs relating to mourning and funerals became more complex, in part a reflection of the greater wealth of the growing middle class. It became a sign of status to have an undertaker take over many of the tasks once done by loved ones.

"You can see a shift in the words that started being engraved on tombstones and used in obituaries," said Loren. "Instead of using the term *died*, people now began falling asleep in the arms of Jesus, storming the gates of heaven, and winning the battle eternal."

Like the Egyptians, the Victorians had elaborate customs relating to death, rituals that were detailed in etiquette books of the day. After someone died, for example, the mirrors in the house were covered, the drapes pulled, and the clocks stopped to mark the moment of their last breath. Female family members wouldn't leave the house until it was time to go to the funeral. The body was kept company in the parlor, even through the night. A piece of black fabric was hung on the front door to indicate someone had died in the house, and postmortem photographs were often taken (children and infants posed in lifelike positions, such as sleeping on a sofa or in a baby buggy). Black-bordered stationery was used by the family after a death, with the width of the border dependent upon who had died—spouses had the widest ribbons, with children and other relatives meriting slightly narrower lines.

The list of rules concerning clothing alone filled many pages, with most of the guidelines applying to women. While the strictures varied somewhat according to the anal-retentiveness of the author, there was a general consensus that a widow should wear deep black for a year and a day, followed by half mourning, when she could wear gray. The mourning guidelines were strictest for widows, but rules existed for a variety of losses. One etiquette guide, for example, listed the mourning period for the death of an infant as six to seven weeks, while that for a child above ten years of age lasted from six months to a year. You should mourn someone who had left you an inheritance for the same amount of time you mourned a grandparent—six months. Siblings merited six to eight months. Given the ubiquity of premature death in this era, some people would have been in mourning almost their entire lives.

Funeral practices also changed, so that by the end of the Victorian era, services that had once been handled by the family and friends became professionalized. "Before the twentieth century, most funerals were held at home," said Loren. "People were typically nursed in their final days by their daughters, and after they died, their bodies were carried to the parlor by their sons. Friends built a wooden coffin and neighbors dug their graves. Everybody knew what to do after someone died, because they'd observed it many times."

Even after funeral directors took over these tasks, part of a growing professionalization of many occupations during the period, strict customs remained, usually determined by the cultural microclimate of a particular locale. Loren recalls the unwritten rules governing funerals in his part of rural Iowa when he was growing up in the 1940s. People could use the hymns "Old Rugged Cross" and "Rock of Ages" at a funeral, but other choices, even the seemingly innocuous "In the Garden," would raise eyebrows. There was a fine line of appropriateness on flowers too: the arrangement shouldn't be too large, but too small wasn't good either. Women were buried in a black or very dark dress, with no pattern in the fabric, while men might get a new tie for the occasion (though people would comment if they'd never seen him wear it while he was breathing).

My conversation with Loren made me realize we're more Victorian than we may think in relation to rituals at the end of life. If you've ever stood before your closet, pondering which black outfit to wear to a funeral, you're following the example of the Victorians. (Many of the customs we associate with mourning, in fact, can be traced to the actions of Queen Victoria as she mourned the loss of her beloved Prince Albert in 1861.) And when we say someone has *passed*—curiously, the *away* part of the phrase has largely disappeared—we echo their delicate phrasing in relation to death. Loren is particularly amused by the euphemism *lost*: as in, a woman has lost her husband. "It always makes me want to ask her if she's looked in all the usual places for him," he told me.

In other ways, though, these Victorian customs have gone the way of the dodo. When we walk down a city street, we have no idea who's in mourning for a recent loss. This isn't entirely a bad thing, of course—all that black must have gotten depressing, especially if you weren't particularly fond of the husband you'd buried and were crossing off the days on the calendar until you could wear gray instead of black. In keeping with the individualism of our age, we can now do anything we please after someone's demise. If you want to dress in scarlet and shoot your husband's ashes up in a fireworks display, you can do it (though some of your friends will likely be creeped out by the thought of cremains falling from the sky onto them).

But I think we lose something, too, as shared rituals become fewer and grief becomes a largely private burden, unnoticed by the larger world except for the brief flurry of Facebook comments after a death is announced. There's comfort to be had in words worn smooth by centuries and in knowing that the prayers said at your mother's demise were also said at the services for your grandparents and great-grandparents. In grieving, it helps to be reminded that humans have been ritualizing death for millennia.

But today, a growing number of people have no service at all. Cremating the body is just the last tidying up of an inevitable biological process, a figurative brushing of the hands.

Which is unfortunate, because funerals can be a jolly good show.

LESSONS FROM THE EXPERTS

Fewer and fewer people know what to do at funerals, according to a woman who works at one of my favorite funeral homes.

It may seem odd to have preferences among mortuaries, but I do. For years I shared the common dislike of the industry—I remember being mordantly interested in Jessica Mitford's *The American Way of Death* as a teenager, tut-tutting at all the greedy villains she gleefully exposes. But the more services I attend, the more grateful I am to have people around who know what to do when someone breathes their last. A compassionate funeral director provides care that lets the family focus on what's most important: putting one foot in front of the other. I've seen this happen multiple times at the funeral home a few blocks from my house. I can't say that it ever feels very homey there, but I do appreciate the assistance its staff provides.

After a service there one day, I found myself standing next to a thirtysomething woman who was gazing at the reception line with a practiced eye.

"Are you a funeral director?" I guessed. When she said she was, I felt like a traveler who'd stumbled upon an English-speaking guide in a foreign country. As the rest of the guests mingled, we professionals—me in a clerical collar, and Deborah in sensible shoes and somber suit—traded stories of what it's like from our side of the death divide.

I was delighted to learn that as a teenager, Deborah had dreadlocks down to her waist and multiple piercings. "People tend to judge you on the basis of appearance, so I had to change my look once I became a funeral director," she said. "But I've always been a bit of a rebel. And it never bothered me to think of death—it's just part of life. I'm unusual in taking an interest in such things, especially as a young person."

According to Deborah, the funeral industry is changing: today more than half of mortuary science students are women. "I think it's a natural fit for women, actually—we tend to be more comfortable relating to people on an emotional level," she said.

It was Deborah who told me that fewer and fewer people know the etiquette of funerals, a decline she's noticed even during her short tenure in the business. They don't know how to express their sympathy for someone who's suffered a loss, for example, or that they're supposed to give hearses right-of-way when they're driving. And many are clueless when they have to plan a service for a loved one, not knowing even the outlines of a memorial ritual or a single faith leader they can contact for help.

Her comments made sense: increasing numbers of people live a significant distance from their extended families and can't travel back for the funerals of great-aunts, second cousins, and other peripheral relatives. Children from divorced families often experience an even greater splintering of familial ties. And fewer people are part of faith communities, which typically include elderly people who have a habit of dying. If all your friends are about the same age, you can go merrily along for quite some time pretending you're immortal. Hearing Deborah's stories made me appreciate all the funerals I've attended of people I didn't grieve deeply, the deceased to whom I've said good-bye with a hail-fellow-well-met attitude. These lessons in death have served me well when it came time for harder losses.

Still, I was impressed to meet someone who had chosen funerals as a career, especially one who didn't mind my curiosity about the day-to-day details of her profession. If my career path had taken a different trajectory, it might well have been me standing there keeping a watchful eye on the reception.

"I love my work," Deborah said. "I'm helping people at one of the hardest times of their lives. And I like how every day is different."

As we chatted, the topic of embalming naturally came up, as I'm sure it often does in conversations with funeral directors. Deborah said that it became popular during the Civil War as a way to preserve bodies to be sent home from battle, but that fewer and fewer people are choosing it today, for which she was grateful because it uses a lot of chemicals. I debated asking her more questions about it, then decided against it as I realized that the cookie I was eating didn't mix well with embalming details. We moved on to cremation, a more antiseptic topic. I asked her what happens to pacemakers (they're removed and recycled) and where you can legally scatter cremains (the short answer is: get permission). And we talked about the differences between religious rituals. After Buddhist funerals, she said that all of the flowers and extra food are typically left behind at the funeral home because it's believed that the soul of the deceased might accompany them if they're carried away. She told how Jews and Muslims have similar practices at the end of life. Both do the washing of the body themselves, with men washing male bodies and women female ones, and in both religions bodies are typically buried without embalming, which is legal as long as the death wasn't from a communicable disease and the body is buried in less than three days (your state laws may differ, so don't blame me if you get into trouble because of the unembalmed body of a relative).

When I asked Deborah if any parts of her job make her uncomfortable, I expected that she'd tell me about preparing a body for viewing or some other detail of dealing with human remains. Instead, she spoke about the growing number of people who look to funeral directors to give them meaning in their grief because they have no spiritual home. "We're here to provide a service," she said. "We're not here to answer the existential questions. It's sad when people look to me for wisdom, because I don't have it."

Clergy, of course, are the ones who are supposed to provide spiritual meaning after a death. If we get virtually everything else wrong, if we give tedious sermons and forget people's names and are sloppy about bookkeeping, usually all is forgiven if we can just provide some comfort to people as they're grieving and dying. Rabbis, imams, deacons, pastors, priests, and shamans know that while they're supposed to help out at all life transitions, the final one is when people typically need them the most.

Even though I dislike wearing a clerical collar (it's uncomfortable and makes people stare at me), I appreciate the fact that sometimes, especially in hospitals and at funerals, it sends a message that transcends the immediate moment. It lets people know that it's not just me saying these words: I'm speaking on behalf of something much larger and older, something big enough to hold whatever grief and despair and anger may be swirling in their hearts.

Many clergy members prefer funerals to weddings, because weddings tend to be high-stress, expensive occasions when the church is more of a stage set than an integral part of the occasion. People generally behave better at memorial services, too, as death tends to bring out the best in people, even ex-spouses and siblings-in-law—though one funeral director did tell me about a service he witnessed during which a fistfight broke out between the deceased's daughters.

Done well, these services can be profoundly comforting and uplifting, a shared ritual of remembering that helps people think not only about the life of the deceased, but also about their own. Many of us, I suspect, have left a funeral resolving to be better people. We're inspired by the life of the deceased—and a little apprehensive about what will be said about us at some unspecified point in the future.

In my own tradition, the Episcopal Church, funerals are our best show. The stately language of the *Book of Common Prayer* blends beautifully with the solemnity of the occasion (the funeral services for the British royals are a particularly good advertisement for my denomination). The service typically begins with the tolling of bells and a procession of people in white robes and vestments walking down the aisle, led by an acolyte holding a brass cross high in the air. As they pace forward in silence, a priest or deacon begins to speak, the words echoing through the church:

> I am Resurrection and I am Life, says the Lord.
> Whoever has faith in me shall have life,
> even though he die.
> And everyone who has life,
> and has committed himself to me in faith,
> shall not die for ever.

Like a costume drama on *Masterpiece Theatre*, the scene is both moving and theatrical. I like the fact, too, that it doesn't make any difference whose life is being honored—whatever the deceased's social standing or bank balance, each gets the same pageantry.

Some funerals are so heart-wrenching, of course, that no one (even me) is making mental observations about how much they resemble a BBC miniseries: one for a teenager who died in a car crash, for example, or for a parent with small children. Often it's the music that carries the most meaning under these circumstances, especially the familiar songs that have been sung as a form of good-bye for centuries, from "Amazing Grace" to "Abide with Me." The food is important, too, because there's nothing like death to make you hungry. Some of the best desserts I've ever eaten have been after a funeral, each bite a reminder that I'm able to savor what the deceased cannot.

Christian services in particular have a lot of references to eternal life, though in the Episcopal Church we tend to let the ritual bear these messages, as many of us think it's unseemly to dwell on them too much in the eulogy. An Episcopal friend of mine, for example, once took me to lunch and said she wanted me to speak at her funeral. "Just don't say that I'm now in heaven," she said. "I hate hearing that at a funeral."

While I hope in my own eventual eulogy there will be multiple references to the good time Lori is having in heaven, I sympathized with her wish. The problem is the facile nature of this sort of rhetoric, which too often speaks with complete assurance of things that are mysteries—the many references in our liturgy to resurrection, salvation, being raised in Christ, and everlasting life, for example, as well as the image of "light perpetual" shining upon the deceased (which makes me wonder how they can ever get a good night's sleep in heaven). Sitting at a funeral one day, I thought back to my time in the Valley of the Kings in Egypt. To anyone who wasn't part of the in-group of Christians at that service, the words of the liturgy must have seemed as incomprehensible as the hieroglyphics painted on the walls of the tombs.

More and more services have no religious language whatsoever, as fewer people are part of faith communities of any kind. Some people have their celebration of life (a term much preferred to the funereal *funeral*) in parks, restaurants, and even bars. I have a friend, for example, who has made plans to hold an event after his passing in a local barbecue joint, with the TVs turned to sports. Anyone who wears a tie will be refused admittance.

As the communal rituals and shared vocabulary of death become less common, one remnant of an earlier time paradoxically looms larger: the eulogy. This summing up of a person's life can be done by a single person or several, but everyone who delivers a eulogy probably spends the night before the service sweating bullets as well as grieving.

I get asked to deliver more than my fair share of eulogies because I'm both a writer and a member of the clergy, a combination that makes me a natural person to speak at a memorial service. While others have the luxury of expressing their grief openly, I have to hold myself together enough to stand up in front of a crowd of people and try to sum up an entire life and spin some comfort out of loss.

Here's a trick I've learned on how to deliver a eulogy without crying. In the margins, I write a to-do list of dull tasks: Finish income taxes. Clean the upstairs closet. Rotate the tires. If I start to get caught up in the emotion of the occasion, I glance at these comments to distract myself. OK, I'm saying good-bye to someone I love, but I really need to do something about the mold in the shower.

I've even officiated at a couple of pet funerals, which is always a challenge in regard to ritual and readings, as most dogs and cats aren't very religious (cats in particular continue to be resentful over no longer being worshiped as gods). At our cat Caesar's burial, for example, I read from a Roman funeral oration from the second century, a literary flourish I doubt he'd have appreciated, though like his namesake, he had no scruples about killing.

The ancient Romans believed that only the most illustrious of the dead merited a funeral oration, but in our modern world, pretty much everyone is deemed worthy. A eulogist gets to deliver the last public words on someone's life, choosing just a few stories and insights that somehow represent an entire existence. It's a humbling challenge.

Some of the best eulogies I've heard have been the shortest. At the funeral of a friend, for example, his three adult children stood up to speak about him. Two were his biological children, while the third was a man in his forties who'd been adopted as a troubled teenager. When it came time for Zach to speak, he was so moved that the only words he could choke out were,

"He changed my life." And those of us sitting in the church who knew his story realized all that was conveyed by those four simple words.

At the other end of the spectrum, my friend Mark, a brilliant and eccentric mathematician who committed suicide, had nearly three hours of stories at his service, a tour de force that gave ample testimony to his many peculiarities and exhausted everyone in attendance. Those stories helped ease the raw and complicated grief that many of us felt at Mark's death. He had friends in several nonoverlapping social networks, so that most of us hadn't known of each other's existence. Coming together for Mark's send-off, we realized how many lives our unusual friend had influenced.

Just as people shouldn't go gentle into that good night, I also think some bling at a funeral can be a good thing. After my death, I've toyed with the idea of having a send-off inspired by my Viking ancestors. Though apparently it's not entirely historically accurate, I do like the idea of having my corpse and my most precious possessions put into a longboat, which would be set out to sea and then set afire by a flaming arrow fired by one of my sons from shore. The expense of this is daunting, however, as well as the fact that I live more than a thousand miles from an ocean.

Deborah the funeral director agrees that many people are looking for new ways to say good-bye. She says that more and more people choose to have some sort of reception with stories and speeches about the deceased but no religious ritual. "I think funeral homes as we know them today are an endangered species," she said. "People find them depressing. Instead we're going to be seeing a lot more sunlit and spacious venues that are for celebrations of life in many forms—weddings, memorial services, parties."

On a trip to Austria, I visited the Vienna Funeral Museum, a cultural institution tailor-made for someone of my predilections. The museum is located in the city's Central Cemetery, one of Europe's finest places to spend eternity. Its exhibits, all done in appropriately somber colors, illustrate the special relationship that the Viennese have with death. For them, all parts of life, including its end, should be celebrated with style.

Elaborate Viennese funerals became popular when the rising middle class of the nineteenth century decided they wanted their own version of the rituals of the nobility. Each step of the process was carefully choreographed to convey the status of the deceased, from the laying out of the body to the cortege leading to the place of burial. Death masks, a plaster cast of a face made just after someone's demise, also became popular as a way to remember the deceased—a version of those postmortem photos of pale-faced infants posed in Victorian baby carriages.

I perked up when I found a jukebox that played the most commonly selected funeral songs in Vienna—a brilliant piece of museum design, I must say. And I peered with great interest at a coffin alarm, which could be triggered by individuals unfortunate enough to be buried alive (a common fear in the Victorian age).

It was all more than a tad morbid but strangely fascinating. The cemetery and museum seemed like a fitting counterpoint, somehow, to the gaiety and elegance of the rest of the city.

In remembering my visit to Vienna, I think of Deborah's speculation that the funeral homes of the future will be restyled as celebration centers. I can see why people want to say goodbye in a setting cheerier than a Victorian manse with dreary wallpaper and velvet curtains. But the Viennese are right, I think, in insisting that a send-off should include both celebration and mourning. Pretending a memorial service is like a wedding, only with the guest of honor abnormally quiet, fools no one. I suspect that not even my New Age friends are totally cheery at funerals. The room may be filled with sunshine, but it's a mistake to deny the shadows that are present as well.

THE VINTAGES OF GRIEF

I got the news of my brother's death while walking down a street in Chicago. The phone call from my sister brought me to a halt in the middle of a busy sidewalk, heedless of the people hurrying past me.

"Alan was found dead by his landlord," my sister said. "He most likely died suddenly. They'll do an autopsy to figure out the cause."

We both knew our brother had been in poor physical shape. Still, my sister's words were an existential shock. I'd seen him just a few days before, during that difficult week when we were helping our mother move into the nursing home.

I was with Bob and our son Carl, and I know I carried on conversations with them for the rest of that afternoon and evening, but I remember virtually nothing of the rest of the day. I had been part of many deaths that I'd anticipated and planned for. Not this one.

In the weeks after Alan's passing, that feeling of unreality persisted. In part because I hadn't seen him very often, I couldn't quite believe he was gone. He loved books and wasn't nearly as enamored of people, but he'd been easy to get along with, not asking much out of life or his siblings. In the busyness of my life it was easy not to think much about him. We'd seen each other at holidays, mainly. We enjoyed our visits, but we weren't close.

And yet how can I say we weren't close, when we shared the same DNA and the same childhood? He was my brother, part of the warp and woof of my family. I grieved his death in part because of the loss of any possibility of a deeper relationship with him. That door had closed forever.

Alan's passing made me realize the unique place that siblings often occupy in our network of relationships. While we begin our lives with deep connections, as adults our paths typically diverge. But when a brother or sister dies, even if we're no longer close, we lose part of our past. There are now just two people who remember the details of my childhood: my sister and me. And frankly, a lot of what I remember is pretty hazy.

My grief shows up at unexpected times, often triggered by seemingly random things—the smell of newly mown hay makes me recall memories of Alan from our childhood on a farm, for example, while the sight of a face similar to his on a passing bus brings tears to my eyes.

During the year after Alan died I came to think of grief as a fine wine, subtly changing with the passage of time. As the losses of middle age accumulate—first a parent, then a sibling, then friends from cancer or accident or suicide—the nuances of mourning become easier to parse. My father's death elicited a mixture of relief and sadness, because his health had declined to the point where there was no hope left for any quality of life. A neighbor's passing brings a sad week but then a lightening of mood; the loss of a young child brings an ache for his parents, triggered each time I pass by their house.

Other times, grief is sharp and overwhelming. When my friend Mark committed suicide, I was angry at him for a full two years, both sorrowful and furious. The day after his funeral, I found my favorite picture of him and tore it methodically into tiny pieces—my grief morphing into a rage that both surprised and frightened me. But gradually those emotions faded, as bit by bit I came to terms with his suicide and the large hole it had left in my family's life. Today my grief for him has mellowed, sipped only occasionally.

The vintage of grief for my brother has its own flavor. It comes and goes, at times sharp and at other times subtle. I find myself thinking of my childhood more than I have in years, like a sea turtle that finds its way back to its home beach after wandering the ocean for thousands of miles.

Because my brother had no spouse or children and had left no instructions about his preferences, my sister and I were left to plan his service. And I, who'd been part of the planning for so many funerals, was at a loss for what to do.

I knew Alan hadn't been a religious person. While I believe that funerals are for the living, and not for the dead, it felt false to do a full Christian service. Instead, after some thought, I planned a simple ritual that we would do just with our immediate family—except, of course, my mother, who had forgotten that her son had died.

We visited her the day of the funeral, and as we talked about trivial matters, I kept thinking of what we were going to do later that afternoon, and how this news would have crushed her just a few months before. I was grateful that she wasn't aware of Alan's death, but at the same time the weirdness of the occasion overwhelmed me. Here we were talking about the weather, and my brother's cremains were in the car outside.

Our cortege of two cars drove from the nursing home to the country cemetery next to the church where we'd grown up. We gathered in the corner where our relatives were buried, and I read a few words from the *Book of Common Prayer*—enough to honor the occasion, I hoped, but not enough to go against the wishes of my brother. We spoke briefly of him and his life. I played Johnny Cash singing "I'll Fly Away" on my iPhone. And then we scattered his ashes on the edge of the cemetery, near the church with the limestone steeple where he'd been baptized, fifty-nine years before.

Sign for the cremation grounds in Crestone, Colorado
(PHOTO CREDIT: BOB SESSIONS)

7

Returning to the Center

Crestone, Colorado

In most towns, a broken-down vehicle wouldn't be taken as a spiritual sign—but most towns aren't Crestone, Colorado.

Bob and I showed up in Crestone after a long drive across the flat-as-a-pancake San Luis Valley, a 5,000-square-mile expanse of high desert in south central Colorado. We passed the turnoff for Great Sand Dunes National Park and Preserve and then drove through mile after mile of irrigated potato fields, grasslands interspersed with rabbitbrush and greasewood, and scattered communities of people eking out a living in one of the poorest parts of the state. The sky was so big that several weather systems were visible at once: huge thunderheads, blue sky, and low-hanging gray clouds each occupied their own corner of the horizon.

Turning off the main highway, we drove for another dozen miles until at last we came to a tiny town at the end of the road: Crestone. Tucked between the grasslands and the sharply rising slopes of the Sangre de Cristo Mountains, this settlement of 150 people was the reason we'd spent two days on the road: it has more spiritual sites per square foot than any other place in North America, including ashrams, temples, monasteries, retreat centers, chapels, labyrinths, and stupas. It's probably the only place in the United States where a ziggurat doesn't look entirely out of place.

It didn't take us long to scope out the town. Its business district consisted of a brewery, a handful of small shops, and a grocery store named Elephant Cloud with a couple of gas pumps out front. I was struck by the architectural contrasts: middle-class homes shared streets with ramshackle cabins and weathered buildings long abandoned. As we headed to the campground north of town, an unattended dog sitting at a curve in the road watched us with alert wariness.

After setting up camp in the national forest, we headed back into town for dinner. I was looking forward to visiting with Kairina Danforth, the mayor of Crestone, whom I'd met on a visit the previous fall when I was touring southern Colorado on a press trip. By the time our group got to town we were behind schedule and so had to zip between several of its spiritual centers at a brisk pace. It was during that all-too-brief visit that I had uttered the single most ridiculous thing I've ever said to a Zen monk: "I've got ten minutes. What can you tell me about Buddhism?"

Happy at the prospect of exploring Crestone at greater leisure, my thoughts were interrupted by Bob's exclamation.

"Damn! The engine light just came on."

Our minivan gave a sigh, a sound that had a vaguely martyred air. We slowed to a crawl.

"What's wrong?"

"I have no idea. But I can barely make it go."

As we inched into the parking lot of the Desert Sage Restaurant, we strategized about what to do. Crestone likely didn't have an auto repair shop, and we'd need to get our vehicle towed to the nearest good-sized town, which was an hour away.

"Just what we need, here in the middle of nowhere," Bob said. "Great timing."

But as we entered the restaurant, we resolved to make the most of the evening. We had towing insurance; we'd figure out the details later. And so we greeted Kairina warmly and a short time later welcomed David Scott, a fellow Crestonian she'd asked to join us. After exchanging pleasantries, I steered the conversation to the reason why we'd traveled nearly a thousand miles from Iowa to this remote location.

"Why is Crestone a center for spirituality?" I asked Kairina and David. "Is there something different about this place, something inherently holy?"

"Well, it's like the broken-wagon-wheel story from Taos," David said. Seeing our puzzled expressions, he continued, "In the 1890s, two artists from the East Coast were passing through New Mexico when a wheel broke on their wagon. They got it fixed in the little village of Taos and liked the place so much they ended up staying there. So now the legend goes that if the mountain wants you to stay there, it will break your car down. Crestone is like that too. If the mountain wants you, it'll find a way to draw you in and keep you here."

"Well, that's interesting," I said. "Our car just broke down, right as we were driving to the restaurant. Does that mean we're supposed to stay?"

Kairina and David exchanged meaningful glances. The implication was clear. Crestone was calling us, and we needed to stay until we answered. Despite my worry about the vehicle, I felt a sense of pride. It's not just everybody who has car trouble in Crestone.

"It's a sign," I told Bob as we returned to our car after our dinner. "You could tell they thought so too."

"A sign of what? We're supposed to move here permanently?" Bob asked.

"A sign that we're supposed to be here."

With Kairina waiting in her car behind us in case she needed to give us a ride to our campsite, Bob turned the key. The engine light was still on, but the vehicle had more power than before. He cautiously eased it out of the parking lot. "I think we're OK on getting back to camp," he said, motioning to Kairina that she could leave.

The next morning, the engine light was off and the van worked fine. Bob thought the transmission had just gotten overheated from driving in the mountains, but he would say that, wouldn't he? As for me, I was grateful for two things: the fact that we didn't have to get it fixed and that our car troubles had opened a door into Crestone.

"It's a Crestone thing," Kairina told me when I relayed the story of the miraculous healing of our van. "That's what we say here when coincidences like this happen. And they happen a lot."

Here's another coincidence: I'd come to Crestone a second time somewhat on a whim, to follow up on my positive first impressions of it the previous year. We were going to be in Colorado anyway, and the town was sort of on the way to where we wanted to go, and I thought the town's reputation for spirituality might have something to offer my exploration of mortality.

So my writer's ears had perked up at dinner when Kairina mentioned that Crestone has the only nondenominational, open-air cremation grounds in the United States. "You don't have to be Buddhist or Hindu to have remains burned here— you just have to be from the area," she explained.

"OK, that seals it." I sent my own meaningful glance in Bob's direction. "We're supposed to be here."

THE MYSTIC'S VISION

As is true of many holy places, you have to *want* to get to Crestone. At 7,500 feet in elevation and bordered by snowcapped mountains, the community is both beautiful and isolated, subject to extremes of weather, wind, and temperature. Bear, elk, and mountain lions live in the surrounding wilderness, while the Baca National Wildlife Refuge in the valley protects nearly 100,000 acres of wetlands and grasslands.

From the 1870s through the 1930s Crestone was a mining town, and then a center for ranching. But its identity underwent a dramatic change in the 1970s when Maurice Strong, a Canadian businessman and United Nations diplomat, and his wife, Danish-born Hanne Marstrand Strong, purchased a 200,000-acre tract of land in the area. Its previous owners had hoped to make the land, known as the Baca Grande Development, into a retirement community. While the Strongs were deciding how to develop it, an elderly local mystic named Glenn Anderson showed up at their door. "I have been waiting for you to arrive," he said, and then explained that Crestone was destined to become an interfaith community where people from all the world's great religions would come to pray, learn, seek answers to the problems of the world, and come to a higher level of spiritual consciousness.

Crestone being Crestone, this information was received not with an escort to the front door, but instead with an invitation to go into more detail. After talking to the man over the course of four days, Hanne went on a vision quest in the mountains to contemplate what she'd heard and then sought additional guidance from elders she knew among the Hopi, a nation with ancestral roots in the San Luis Valley. Guided by their affirmation and her own intuition that the mystic had spoken the truth, she moved forward with plans to make his vision a reality. She and her husband established the nonprofit Manitou Foundation, which began donating land to religious groups that agreed to establish centers there. One by one they came: Buddhists, Hindus, Christians, and seekers who followed a wide range of other paths. They built retreat centers, chapels, meditation halls, and religious landmarks ranging from stupas to labyrinths. Within a decade, remote Crestone had become an international spiritual mecca.

But in my conversations with local residents, many said that Crestone has been a power center for millennia. They told me about the immense aquifer that lies beneath the town, its water sitting atop a crystalline formation that some believe amplifies the vibrational energy in the area. Before white people came to the area, they said, it was known as the Bloodless Valley, a haven where members of different tribes could safely meet.

Such claims are difficult to prove, of course, but it's certainly true that the valley is filled with archaeological sites dating back thousands of years. And Mount Blanca, located sixty miles to the south of Crestone near the Great Sand Dunes, is regarded as one of the four sacred mountains of the Navajo and Hopi Nations. To them it is Sisnaajini (Eastern Mountain Where the Light Comes into the World).

And as further proof that there's something in this place that makes people think of spiritual matters, even the name of the nearby mountain range has religious significance. Early Spanish explorers named it the Sangre de Cristo, or Blood of Christ Mountains, after the red glow that often lights the peaks at sunset.

I remembered what Kairina had told me when Bob and I joined her for dinner on our first night in Crestone. "We're the spiritual heart of North America," said Kairina. "Some people think we always have been."

While Crestone has just 150 residents, the surrounding county has about 1,500, most of whom live in the Baca Grande subdivision, known as the Baca by residents. The majority of the spiritual centers line a gravel road that marks the border between a residential area and the Rio Grande National Forest that covers the foothills of the Sangre de Cristo Mountains.

As Bob and I drove through the winding gravel lanes of the Baca, we saw how the architectural quirkiness of Crestone reaches its full flower in this subdivision. While people have to get a permit to build, the county doesn't have many regulations on *how* things get constructed. As a result, the buildings are a glorious hodgepodge of architectural styles, from straw bale houses where hobbits would feel right at home to high-end Southwestern-style mansions. One house had a yard full of statues ranging from the Virgin Mary to Taoist sages, for example, as well as a labyrinth, Norwegian trolls, and meditation seats where visitors can Zen out, surrounded by hundreds of crystals.

No matter where you are in the Baca, a holy site isn't far away. We did a circumambulation of a Buddhist stupa, a tall structure filled with holy relics, and visited the Nada Hermitage, a Carmelite retreat center with a sunlit chapel and cabins beautifully constructed of adobe. After paying our respects to Lakshmi (the Hindu goddess of prosperity and purity) at the Haidakhandi Universal Ashram, we climbed Crestone's ziggurat, a structure modeled after the ancient temples of Babylon. Later that afternoon we marveled at the beauty of a kiva—an underground sacred chamber—built in the style of the Pueblo Indians.

On my previous visit, I had visited the Vajra Vidra, one of several Tibetan Buddhist retreat centers in the area. Our guide there had said that Crestone's high-desert landscape framed by mountains reminds many Tibetans of their homeland. In Himalayan culture, it's considered auspicious to locate a monastery in such a landscape because the peaks' local deities can serve as protectors for the sacred space. In Crestone, he said, the nearby mountains shelter many people doing retreats, including a number who are doing the arduous three-year meditation retreat that's the gold standard of Tibetan Buddhist practice.

When I mentioned this to Kairina, she nodded. "Many of the spiritual centers here have practitioners on extended retreats," she said. "One of our more unusual occupations, in fact, is retreat master—the people who provide for their physical needs while they're meditating, like food and drink."

As we explored Crestone, my thoughts often turned to those brave spiritual adventurers in the mountains above me. My own fledgling meditation practice was inching forward. I prided myself on the fact that most days I was able to sit in silence for twenty minutes. But what would it be like to meditate day after day, month after month, year after year? For me, certainly, it would be crazy making. But if you want to meditate for three years, this Little Tibet seemed like a good place to do so, in this quiet oasis with its sweeping views of the San Luis Valley, the Sangre de Cristos at your back, and that aquifer of water sitting atop a crystal underneath. And maybe, perhaps, some local mountain deities keeping watch over you as well.

The brewery and coffee shop were easy places to start conversations with the locals—in such a small community, visitors provide a welcome change of pace. We met people who had lived in Crestone for years and others who'd recently moved to town. It's a hard place to make a living, they said, but something about the place makes it worth it.

"I think a lot of us show up in Crestone and realize, 'This is the place I've been searching for all my life,'" one person told me.

One afternoon at the coffee shop, I was pleased to meet Hanne Strong, the woman who answered the door to the mystic in 1978, setting in motion a chain of events that had changed the town's history. She told me how pleased she was with how his initial vision had unfolded and of future plans for the area, including developing a pilgrimage route that would run from Crestone to Mount Blanca.

"Despite our isolation, people find their way here," she said. "We get about twenty thousand visitors a year, with nine thousand of them doing a retreat of some sort at one of our centers. Crestone has become a school of the spirit—that was the mystic's original vision, and I'm delighted at the ways it's become a reality."

Later that afternoon, I met another community elder: John P. Milton, an ecologist, author, and retreat leader who founded the Way of Nature, a program that offers meditation retreats and wilderness quests around the world. Based in Crestone, John has helped thousands of people deepen their connection to nature and spirituality through practices gleaned from a variety of traditions.

Bob and I met John at the Thoreau-like cabin in the woods bordering North Crestone Creek where he has lived on and off for nearly forty years. As we followed him on a tour around the property, the gray-haired John using a staff as he trod the rough ground, I felt as if we were walking with a modern-day John Muir.

Resisting the urge to brag about the fact that our van had broken down on our first night in Crestone, I told him about my quest to come to terms with mortality by visiting sacred places. I mentioned a comment David Scott had made on our first evening in town—many people here, he said, had died before they died, meaning that they'd undergone some serious illness or deep suffering that had propelled them on the spiritual path.

The phrase clearly resonated with John, in part because of his own near-death experience. He told of being struck by lightning when he was forty-six, and of how he spent six hours suspended in a state between life and death. "That time gave me a sense for the clear, underlying light that I think we all experience when we die," John said. "When I returned to my body, I realized that most of what I'd thought was important really wasn't."

Most people don't have that dramatic of an experience, of course. But John said many people sign up for his programs as a way of coming to terms with mortality. He pointed toward a nearby clearing, where a dozen tents were set up for the participants in his current program. "Often they're dealing with their own aging, or the loss of someone they love," he said. "That's a common time to want to go deeper."

He described the various practices that he teaches, from Qigong to Taoist meditation, but then he admitted that the heart of his instruction is simply giving people the chance for extended time out-of-doors. "The more connections you make to the natural world, the more your inner blockages begin to be transformed," he said. "You begin to see things from a much longer perspective. You get a sense for the immense geologic sweep of time and realize how small you and your problems are. And I think something happens at a very deep, cellular level when we come in contact with the wildness of nature— for millions of years we've been tuned to that resonance, and returning to it is transformative and deeply healing."

I thought of my time among the Maori, who call themselves *tangata whenua*, people of the land. John's words were entirely consistent with their beliefs. And seeing the way he looked around this piece of land tucked into a bend of the creek, I guessed John also felt a deep, loving kinship with its trees, rocks, and water. I was beginning to experience some serious envy of the people who were going to spend a couple of weeks in the company of this man.

"There's a huge longing in our culture for a connection to spirit, but many people are so alienated from themselves, and from nature, that they don't know how to respond," John continued. "Connecting with the natural world is the oldest of all spiritual paths. No matter what your religious affiliation, this path is open to you. You can learn about life and death just by seeing the fallen trees returning to earth and the mushrooms growing after a rain. The earth is always willing to teach us, if we just pay attention."

ZEN AND THE ART OF CREMATION

There was one more person I needed to talk to in Crestone: Christian Dillo, the German-born Zen monk who serves as a resident teacher at the Crestone Mountain Zen Center, the man who made such a strong impression on me during my first visit. Recalling our meeting, I appreciated how he hadn't made me feel stupid when I gave him a ten-minute time limit on our conversation. "The time we have together is what we have," he'd said in classic Zen fashion. "Let us make it enough." I was eager to learn more from this man with the intense gaze and serene manner.

After driving up a winding and bumpy gravel road past stands of juniper, pinyon, and ponderosa pines, Bob and I were greeted at the entrance to the center by Christian, who was dressed in Western-style clothes except for a bib-like garment known as a *rakusu*. Worn around the neck, it symbolizes the robe worn by the Buddha as well as the vows the person has taken to follow Buddhist precepts.

"Come to the teahouse," Christian said. "It's a good place to talk."

Situated in an enclosed courtyard next to a dry Zen garden with artfully placed rocks, the tiny wooden house was cozy and peaceful. Inside, Christian lit a stick of incense and invited us to sit on the tatami mats that lined the floor. Silence fell. I appreciated the fact that I didn't have to fill it immediately (one of the benefits of being around monks, I've learned, is that conversations typically flow at a slower pace). I savored the austere lines of the room and the pleasant aroma of the incense.

"How can I help you?" Christian finally asked.

I explained about my writing project, telling him of my brother's death, my mother's dementia, and my travels around the world trying to make sense of them. I'd been drawn to Crestone without knowing quite why, I said, but thought it might have something to do with its cremation ground.

"What do you think about it?" I asked. "Is it a good thing for the community?"

Christian, it turned out, was the perfect person to answer these questions, because he'd been on the town's planning and zoning commission when the cremation ground was proposed. I took a moment to appreciate the image of a Zen monk serving on a planning and zoning commission, then listened to his story.

"It was quite contentious at first," he recalled. "People had all sorts of concerns, including possible harmful emissions and the danger of sparks starting fires. But it's now become an accepted, and I think a valuable, part of life here."

The first cremation was done in 2008 on a site established and maintained by volunteers from the Crestone End of Life Project. At each one, the fire department stands guard to make sure the fire is kept under control. While people mark the ritual in a variety of ways, most often with drumming or singing, one element has become a tradition: each person in attendance places a juniper branch on the pyre.

"Most of the time in the West, cremations are done in secret, in places removed from the living," Christian said. "But other parts of the world have long recognized that this final death ritual should be open to those on a serious spiritual path.

From a Buddhist point of view, cremations provide a powerful teaching. Death, after all, is the ultimate lesson in impermanence. So I think it's a good thing to have this here. During a cremation, you can look around at people's faces and see how strong the experience is for them. You look at the body being cremated and you can feel the elemental power. You get it in your bones that this body is now gone."

We sat in silence some more. As the scent of the incense drifted through the room, I watched the smoke waft from the end of the stick and wondered what it would be like to see a body being burned.

Turning to less intense topics, I brought up something that had been bothering me. I'd spoken to a number of Crestone residents who were ambivalent about having attention drawn to it by the media, namely me. They feared it would become too popular, another trendy site for the spiritually adventurous. (So let me insert a Crestone public service announcement: it's hard to get to, the winters are harsh, jobs are scarce, and the mosquitoes can be ferocious.)

Reflecting his background in the no-nonsense traditions of both Germany and Zen, Christian was skeptical of the idea that Crestone is inherently special. And when I brought up the water-on-top-of-crystal theory, he looked at me with the same sort of patient but long-suffering expression he'd used when I'd given him a ten-minute limit to our conversation.

"I don't know what Crestone is; I choose to look at it like any other mountain town," he said, then backtracked a bit. "The remoteness is unusual, and the wildness of the land. We crave a connection to the wild—it reminds us of our shared embodied heritage with all living beings. And life is so precious here. This high alpine desert is surprisingly fragile. It's not like a jungle that grows back quickly. If you disturb the earth, it can take a hundred years for it to return to what it was."

Most of all, Christian said, people respond to the quiet. "That's what people notice most when they come here: how silent it is. We crave places like this. The problem is that they're easier than ever before to get to, but the more people who go to them, the more they lose what draws us to them. It's a terrible paradox."

Unfolding his long legs with graceful ease, Christian stood up and invited us to join him for lunch. As we walked to the dining hall we began to chat about less weighty matters. I told him that I was learning how to meditate from an app on my phone and asked him what he, as a professional Buddhist, thought about that.

"You should use whatever works," he said. "But at a certain point, you might want to get a teacher. A good teacher speeds up the path."

Over a lunch of tofu and salad grown in the center's gardens, he elaborated, talking about his reservations about how trendy the concept of mindfulness has become. He was leery of it being reduced to just a technique that people used to de-stress. "Mindfulness is a powerful practice," he said, "but many people want to improve their life without transforming it. That's not really Buddhism."

"So what is the heart of Buddhist teaching?" I asked, then added, "This time I can give you more than ten minutes."

His smile told me he remembered our initial encounter. "Perhaps this: suffering equals pain times resistance. When pain is zero, suffering is zero, but we cannot get rid of pain once and for all, because to be a human body is to feel pain. The other factor is resistance. Unlike pain, it is in our control. Through meditation, you can learn to allow your experience as it is, to lessen your resistance. In Zen, in fact, some pain is part of the practice. When you do zazen, your legs hurt, your back aches, but if you learn to make space for those sensations and be kind to them, you will still feel the pain but you won't suffer."

Seeing my raised eyebrows, he added, "At least not as much."

He offered the corollary as we stood up to begin our leave-taking: "Suffering can also come from grasping at pleasure. We suffer because we want to cling to it, to keep it from disappearing. But like pain, pleasure will pass as well. We can learn not to attach to either of them."

Christian's words echoed in my mind as we headed back into town, retracing our route down the steep gravel road and then making our way to the brewery in the middle of Crestone. Our week here—a time period that felt both much shorter and much longer than seven days—was ending. I hoped our van would have enough oomph to take us out of town the next morning, but at the same time I was sorry at the thought of leaving.

I watched as a man walked past me into the brewery wearing a bright green plush bathrobe, his legs and feet bare underneath. That's so Crestone, I thought, and smiled.

In the late afternoon, we drove to the cremation ground, heading out of town for several miles and turning right at a sign that bore a single word: Pyre. The old-fashioned word was evocative of much older traditions, from pyres on the banks of the Ganges River in India to pre-Christian funeral rites in the British Isles. Fire has always been an essential part of religious ceremonies. Add the element of death and you have a powerful combination indeed.

To be honest, I was bracing myself for my first sight of the cremation ground. As much as I appreciated the homemade aesthetic of many of the buildings here—as well as the creative reuses of old school buses—I mentally prepared myself for the fact that this place might be simply depressing and ramshackle.

Instead, I found it deeply moving.

The sign at its entrance set the tone: "You have entered a sacred space," it read. "Please enter this place with reverence, honoring those whose lives were celebrated here."

A circular fence of bamboo surrounded the site, with a half-dozen openings into an inner courtyard. Stepping inside, my eyes were immediately drawn to the structure in the center: a rectangular platform made of heat-resistant bricks, about three feet high and ten feet long. There were scorch marks on it, but no other sign of its use. Brilliantly blooming yellow flowers filled the rest of the space, their stalks swaying gently in the wind. I thought of the Day of the Dead altars filled with marigolds, another flower the color of sunshine.

Walking the perimeter, I read the handcrafted copper plaques nailed to the posts. Each featured the name of someone who had been cremated here; most also contained some other design as well, from an Irish harp to a yin-yang symbol. Above the fence, I could see the Sangre de Cristo Mountains in the distance, their peaks obscured by late-afternoon clouds. The site was silent except for the muted sound of the wind.

It wasn't grim or depressing at all; instead it felt like liminal space. It was different, somehow, from the rest of Crestone, existing in a betwixt-and-between place, on the border between prairie and mountain and life and death.

I remembered Kairina's description of the final days of her husband, Harold Danforth, a death that seemed as perfect a send-off into eternity as I could imagine. During the last six weeks of his life, volunteers from the Crestone End of Life Project had provided support and comfort to both of them. After his passing, they helped her wash and anoint his body, which was kept at home for three days, a period during which friends and loved ones came to pay their respects. He was never left alone, even at night, harking back to much older traditions. Very early on the morning of the third day, his body was transported to the cremation site, and as the first fingers of dawn started to be visible on the horizon, the fire was lit.

"It was in winter, so the air was cold, and the scene was very somber," Kairina remembered. "But the fire brought warmth and light, and gradually the mood shifted. Everyone was given a branch of juniper and came forward to place it on the pyre, and then people came forward one by one to share stories about my husband. There was drumming and singing and clapping. The cremation took about two hours, and by the end of it the mood had changed. It was almost a kind of alchemy. I felt enveloped in love and compassion. The entire process helped me move beyond my grief into a place of acceptance and even joy."

As I was leaving the cremation ground, I chose an exit at random, one in the general direction of our van. Before I left the courtyard, I stopped for one last look at the pyre, trying to imprint upon my mind this remarkable sacred site blending death and life, this place adorned by brilliant yellow flowers and watched over by the brooding peaks of the Sangre de Cristos.

Then I turned and saw a plaque, one of the many nailed to the fence. The name on it startled me: Davita Decorah. Decorah was the name of the small Iowa town where I'd grown up. And there it was, the last thing I saw as I left the enclosure.

It goes without saying that this was a Crestone thing. But I think it was more than that: it was a reminder that in some inexplicable way, the cremation ground is my home too.

A gravestone in a pioneer cemetery in Iowa (PHOTO CREDIT: LORI ERICKSON)

8

Resting in Peace

Graveyards

A cocktail reception in a mausoleum? Why, yes, I'd love to attend.

My fellow travel writers and I got the invitation from Milwaukee's Forest Home Cemetery, a graveyard so beautiful that it's a tourist attraction in its own right. I could tell some of my colleagues were uneasy, their eyes flitting frequently to the entrance as they sipped their drinks, but the rest of us were having a wonderful time.

"Can you believe we're drinking in a *mausoleum*?" I said to them as we clinked our glasses with enthusiasm.

Which pretty much sums up the difference in opinion about graveyards: either you think they're fascinating, or you hope to enter one only after you're dead.

For the former group, Milwaukee's Forest Home is a destination cemetery. It's also an example of how the Victorians revamped more than mourning customs during the nineteenth century: they upgraded graveyards as well.

In prior centuries, most people were buried haphazardly in municipal plots, with no record of individual graves and no attempt to keep families together. Church members had a more dignified final resting place: those of highest social or religious status were interred underneath the floor of the building, those of lesser rank in the area just outside the church, and the lowest classes near the exterior wall of the churchyard. Individuals who had committed suicide (which was considered a mortal sin) were on the other side of the wall entirely. But as the years passed, this solution proved problematic, as more and more bodies were piled on top of each other. During floods, the coffins sometimes broke open and bodies emerged on the surface—a source of contamination for water supplies, as well as a disadvantage when the church was trying to attract new members.

In the early nineteenth century, during the era when people started sleeping instead of dying, graveyards became *cemeteries*—a term derived from the Greek word for dormitory. And no-frills burial grounds started to be replaced by green, wooded enclaves on the outskirts of cities, with graves marked by elaborate statuary and bordered by decorative trees, bushes, and flowers, many of them exotic and imported species, so that the grounds became a botanical garden as well as a place for bodies. At a time when most urban areas were dusted with soot, packed with people, and filled with the stench of garbage and excrement, this new style of cemetery beckoned the living as well as the dead. The first garden cemetery in the United States was Mount Auburn Cemetery near Cambridge, Massachusetts, created in 1831, setting a fashion that was emulated in places that included Laurel Hill in Philadelphia, Bellefontaine in St. Louis, Oakland in Atlanta, Graceland in Chicago—plus Forest Home in Milwaukee.

Wealthy Episcopalians established Forest Home in 1850, wanting an appropriately dignified spot for their earthly remains. They bought seventy-four wooded acres on the outskirts of the city and planned a cemetery that would be a public park as well as a place for the deceased (the Episcopalians allowed others to buy plots if they had enough cash). They envisioned it as a place to savor the genteel and poignant pleasures of contemplating one's mortality, a favorite pastime of the Victorians.

Through the next decades, Forest Home flourished as the moneyed citizens of the city competed to erect ever-grander markers. "From the 1870s through the turn of the century, Forest Home was the scene of a monumental outbreak of one-upmanship," writes John Gurda in *Cream City Chronicles: Stories of Milwaukee's Past.* "Obelisks, pyramids, crosses, columns, and spheres sprouted like mushrooms after a rain, each larger than the last."

A liquor wholesaler put up an eighty-four-ton stone pillar bearing a statue of a Greek goddess. Emil Blatz, a brewer, topped him with a five-hundred-ton mausoleum with a tiled roof and marble walls. It stood across the lane from the monuments of two other Milwaukee brewing dynasties, the Pabst and the Schlitz families, creating a triad that was inevitably dubbed the Beer Baron Corner. A staff of fifty men tended the grounds of Forest Home, which included ornamental ponds, fountains, elaborate gardens, and seventeen miles of footpaths and carriageways. Tame deer and peacocks added to the pastoral serenity.

The people of Milwaukee—even the ones who couldn't afford to have loved ones buried there—flocked to the cemetery for relaxation and entertainment, taking the streetcar line that had been constructed to it. On weekends the grounds were so crowded that tickets were sold; one Sunday afternoon eight thousand people showed up to stroll under the trees.

After hearing about the cemetery's history from our guide, I took another sip of Milwaukee-brewed beer, grateful for the welcome this City of the Dead has long extended to visitors.

Back home, I realized that my hometown has its own version of a garden cemetery: Oakland, a tree-lined oasis that's been accepting the remains of Iowa Citians since 1843. On an unseasonably hot day in June when the temperature was forecast to be in the 90s, I packed several bottles of water, snacks, and a couple of books on death (conveniently, my shelves are full of them) and drove to Oakland Cemetery in a historic neighborhood of the city. I would spend the day contemplating mortality.

I hoped to have some company, because the previous day I'd sent an email to a dozen friends with this in the subject line: "An Invitation to Talk About Mortality." I'll be in the cemetery from nine to five, I told them. Stop by if you want to talk about death.

It's an indication of the peculiar nature of my social circle that several people accepted my invitation. (Though another declined with the reply, "Are you kidding? It sounds like a foretaste of hell.") I found a gazebo in the corner of the cemetery where cremains of bodies donated to the local medical school are interred, set up my lawn chair, got comfortable, and started thinking. Despite the heat of the day, a breeze kept me relatively cool. Periodically friends came by and we talked. But mainly I simply sat and observed the quiet rhythms of life here. Occasionally a jogger ran past. A couple of teenagers whizzed by on skateboards. A pregnant woman walked slowly past me, her large stomach silhouetted against the gravestones behind her. Late in the day, an elderly woman drove up and took out a watering can from her trunk. She filled it at a hydrant, then hauled it to a grave near her car and watered its flowers. She repeated the process three times, her methodical movements giving me the impression she'd done this many times.

Loren Horton had told me that graveyards are fruitful places to study history—each part of them has something to teach us, he said, from the design of the entrance gate and style of landscaping to the shape and type of material used for markers. For example, slate was common in eighteenth-century New England because it was often locally quarried and easy to carve, while farther west, limestone predominated. The Victorians favored marble, though bronze and iron were also popular. Today the most common material is granite, which withstands weathering better than marble and can be easily etched with machine or laser tools. Finely detailed portraits are now the fashion in many locales. Once only the very wealthy could preserve their image for eternity; now it's a middle-class option.

My friends the ancient Egyptians left their mark on cemeteries too—obelisks and pyramids were common adornments in nineteenth-century graveyards and still dominate the silhouettes of many graveyards. Angels, on the other hand, usually wear Greek or Roman dress, and populate cemeteries in such numbers that I wonder if they're neglecting their duties somewhere else.

The Victorians used a wide variety of symbols that once conveyed a great deal of information to passersby, though we've largely lost the ability to read them. An intact column means that the deceased lived to a ripe age; a broken one indicates that the person died prematurely. Crosses come in many variations that indicate denomination and ethnic background, from the Greek cross of the Orthodox to St. Andrew's cross for those of Scottish descent. Lambs adorn many tombstones for children, while a dove carrying a rosebud in its beak means that an infant rests beneath the marker.

Thanks to Loren, I could see how much the cemetery was influenced by fashion: keeping up with the Joneses doesn't end just because the Joneses are dead. I remembered the beer barons one-upping each other in Milwaukee and the way obelisks started multiplying like mushrooms in the nineteenth century. Today, laser-etched portraits are all the rage; tomorrow it may be memory chips embedded in markers, ones that beam out a hologram if someone passes by, similar to the scene in *Star Wars* where a recorded Princess Leia tells Obi-Wan Kenobi he's her only hope.

So-called green cemeteries are gaining in popularity as well. A number of my fellow citizens in Iowa City are agitating for one, a natural addition to a community that takes recycling seriously. Instead of cremation, which requires a large amount of energy, or embalming a body and putting it into a casket and then a vault—a procedure that uses a cocktail of potent chemicals and a lot of space—the body is wrapped in a cloth or other biodegradable covering and placed in a grave. Many green burial sites gradually become forests, the trees drawing nourishment from what's buried underneath. If the whole Viking-longboat-with-flaming-arrow thing doesn't work out, I reflected that I might do this instead, because spending my afterlife as a maple tree sounds appealing. I recalled the Mexican shaman's comment that we all owe Mother Earth a body for what we've taken from her during our lives. Coming back as a tree might just settle the debt.

As I strolled through the cemetery that day, I explored my personal history as well as that of the community. I found the grave of the surgeon who'd repaired a hernia years ago ("my guts are still minding their p's and q's, thanks to you," I told her) and the grave marker of the ex-husband of a friend. I remembered the afternoon when we gathered to bury his ashes, recalling the low roar of his motorcycle-riding friends as they showed up to honor him and the feel of dirt in my hand as I threw a handful of soil onto the box containing his remains. I saw the monument for a former landlord, surprised to see that next to it was the grave of his ten-year-old daughter. During the years I lived in his apartment, I didn't realize the sadness that he must have carried within him.

Even if I didn't have a connection to the deceased, I read the epitaphs with curiosity. Loren had said that in the colonial era, they often served as a warning to the living: "As I am now so shall you be; prepare for death and follow me" was a common cheery message, for example. Most of the ones I saw that day didn't bother to sermonize but simply gave a few details about the person's life. When you're paying for chiseled words on marble, you don't want to get too chatty, and terse Mother, Father, Husband, and Wife were most common. But I spotted more unusual descriptors as well. One woman was buried beneath a stone marked "Professor." Another couple wanted to make sure that passersby realized they weren't from around here: "Born in Germany," it said under the man's name, and "Born in Brooklyn, New York" under the wife's. No mention of where they died, but I guessed they were disappointed if they breathed their last in Iowa City.

Back in my lawn chair once again, driven into the shade by the growing heat of the day, I was happy to have a friend show up. For an hour Wendy and I talked about growing older. Recently retired, she was struggling to find a new identity now that she was no longer employed. She spoke of how difficult it was to sort through the boxes of books and papers she had accumulated in her career and how she was debating where she would live in advanced old age. These sorts of conversations come naturally in this setting, I realized, as we begin to contemplate joining our comrades buried around us.

An hour later, William showed up and told me that during part of his childhood, his father was a mortician. They lived in a funeral home—a detail that I hadn't known despite being friends for years. It made him comfortable with death, William said, and contributed to his decision to become a physician.

Next came Jody, arriving by bike despite the heat. She shared the story of a letter she received from her mother a year after she died: it was in her mother's handwriting, she recalled, and had been mailed a few days before. She thinks it must have slipped into some nook or cranny in the nursing home and been mailed by a staff member once it was discovered. She described the moment it arrived and the sense of unreality as she received a message from the Great Beyond.

"In the letter she told me how much she loved me," she said, blinking back tears.

"Maybe it really did come from your mother after her death," I said.

We sat in silence as we pondered the mechanics of how the dead might communicate with the living.

Before the two of them left, William told a final story. The previous day, when he was visiting his parents in a nursing home, he passed by two elderly women sitting in wheelchairs in the hallway. They were holding hands but not talking.

William stopped to greet them. "How are you doing today?" he asked.

"We're waiting to die," one of them said.

I recalled other cemeteries I'd visited through the years, the American Cemetery above the beach at Normandy where thousands lost their lives on D-day, and the military cemetery in South Dakota where Bob's parents are buried. My father-in-law's time in the Navy during World War II had earned both him and his wife a spot among the immaculately kept, orderly rows.

Ironically, those who've taken religious vows are often buried in similarly regimented fashion. Many of the cemeteries at monasteries are lined with identical markers, the occupants buried in the order of their deaths. Other religious groups follow this pattern as well. Iowa's Amana Colonies, a former communal society, traditionally buried its members in the order of their deaths under modest markers. This pattern posed a problem, though, when the community wanted to honor Christian Metz, their beloved leader who died in 1867. An ostentatious monument would be inappropriate, but they wanted to mark his role in nurturing the society for decades. The solution was to give him two burial plots, so that his is the only marker that's slightly off center as one gazes down the rows.

In one sense cemeteries are great equalizers—everyone here rests in similar silence, no matter what their social or economic background—but in other ways they reveal the perennial divisiveness of humanity. Religious divisions are often extended into graveyards, with Catholics barring Protestants (and vice versa). In Vienna, I remembered, the oldest part of the Jewish section was ragtag and overgrown with greenery—a reflection, perhaps, of the fact that the family members who would have tended the graves perished during the Holocaust. And today the establishment of Muslim cemeteries generates controversy in some communities.

Part of the reason for this, of course, is that cemeteries contain not only the dead—they draw the living as well. Having one in your part of town means that you're going to get visitors, even if they don't come partying on Day of the Dead. In years past, Decoration Day (May 30) was the time to bring flowers to graves in many communities, a practice that later became incorporated into Memorial Day. When Loren Horton was small his parents would go from one graveyard to the next on Decoration Day, telling him stories of his many dead relatives at each stop. He traces his interest in history to the ways in which the past was brought to life in these stories.

"This custom of leaving things on graves is very culture specific," he said. "The Chinese, for example, leave food at grave markers. I remember hearing a Chinese woman chided once for this practice by someone who told her that the dead couldn't eat. 'They can't smell the flowers that you leave either,' she replied."

Jews have a custom I like very much: when they visit a grave, they place a pebble or stone on the marker. I remember visiting my friend Teri's grave and being pleased that the rock I carried in my pocket (a worry stone I'd picked up on a beach in New Zealand) exactly fit an indentation on her marker. I appreciated being able to leave something that will last, unlike flowers.

Coins are the memorial token of choice at the spot where the music died—the Iowa cornfield where a small airplane carrying musicians Buddy Holly, Ritchie Valens, and J. P. Richardson, "the Big Bopper," crashed on February 3, 1959. Don McLean used the tragedy as the basis for his "American Pie" song, the one with the chorus that's impossible to get out of your head once you hear it. Before boarding the plane, Ritchie Valens flipped a coin with guitarist Tommy Allsup to see who would take the seat and who would follow by bus. Valens won the toss and lost his life. To this day, pilgrims come from around the world to leave coins at the marker where he died.

And I recall a display at the National Museum of Anthropology in Mexico City that re-creates the burial of a Neanderthal man. He rests on his side as if he is sleeping, and scattered all around him are flowers.

YOUR MORTALITY IS CALLING

The first time Flora from China offered me a free casket, I laughed. "We are a company specialized in wooden casket field, with good quality and pretty competitive price," she wrote to me via email. "FREE SAMPLES will be sent for your evaluation!"

I hit delete, adding it to my mental tally of weird messages I've received courtesy of maintaining a website devoted to spiritual travels. Over the years I've gotten queries on how to join the Salem witches and how to apologize for something one did in a previous life, for example, as well as a message from a Catholic priest in India asking whether I could wrangle him a complimentary hotel at Lourdes ("I'm willing to do confessions for free," he wrote).

The second time Flora contacted me, I was intrigued enough to click on the message's attachment, which described the thirty-eight models her company produced. She was right: their prices *were* reasonable. I could get a handsome elm casket with velvet interior for $568. Even solid mahogany wasn't that much more expensive, and a flimsy box meant for cremation could be had for as little as $198. I didn't know the going rate for an American-made casket, but I was sure it was considerably higher.

The third time I got a message from Flora, a month after the first, a tinge of paranoia kicked in. She couldn't have known I was writing a book about death, could she? I knew Google reveals all sorts of information to businesses looking for online customers, but this sort of direct pitch was far more intrusive than a little ad tucked at the bottom of the page. What did Flora know about me? Why was she named Flora, when her last name was clearly Chinese? Would she actually send me a casket from China? How would she ship it? Would it arrive via the postman or FedEx? What would I do with it once it arrived? I'd read of people using handcrafted caskets as coffee tables in the interim period between making them and using them, but this had always struck me as a trend with no staying power, as few of us want to be reminded of our mortality every time we walk through the living room.

But my most persistent question was this: did Flora know something I didn't?

Personal emails from Chinese casket manufacturers are unusual, but reminders of our mortality come in many forms. Physicians deliver many of these messages, which are often couched in the language of medical tests and cancer survival statistics. But graveyards deliver their own silent messages, too, as we drive past them on our way to work and school, to appointments with our hairdressers and coffee dates with friends. We may not know the finer points of the symbolism on the markers, but they carry a message nevertheless. We'll wait for you, they say. Take your time. We're patient.

The heyday of the grand garden cemeteries is long gone. More and more people are cremated, their ashes scattered off of docks and boats and at scenic spots in the mountains. Many cemeteries now insist upon modest little markers that can be easily mowed around. The impressive cities of the dead, the enclaves with ornate gates and beautiful statuary and lush landscaping, have been redesigned for maximum efficiency. I suspect that few angels clad in flowing robes care to visit even briefly.

In many ways this is a good thing, of course, for all those accoutrements are expensive and take up a lot of land. But we lose something, too, I think, when there are no markers to indicate that someone has lived, breathed, loved, and died. I thought of the woman with her watering can, coming back to the grave every few days to make sure the flowers were healthy. I pictured Loren Horton walking through the cemetery, gaining insights into history and sociology from each marker. And I remembered how it was to contemplate mortality amid the rustling of tree leaves and twittering of birds, in a quiet corner of the cemetery where I could see the tendrils of life and death intertwine.

THE LAST RIDE

When Hugh Wingo died at the age of ninety-six, his daughter Marian had him embalmed and put into a cardboard box. She pulled up her van to the delivery area of her local funeral home and watched as the attendants placed him in the back, where the seats had been taken out. Then she drove two days across Mississippi, Alabama, Georgia, and South Carolina before finally reaching his family home of West Jefferson, North Carolina—a seven-hundred-mile journey that they had planned together before his death.

"I wanted to have one last trip with my dad," she explained to me.

The two of them had traveled together a lot through the years, including many times on that same route. They knew which rest stops were the cleanest, where the McDonald's restaurants were, and which barbecue joints had the best ribs. The oddest thing about the trip, according to Marian, was that her dad was silent—a rare occurrence when he was alive.

"I talked more on that trip than on any other journey we'd taken," she recalls. "I told him what we were passing—'This is where we stopped for coffee on our way to see Aunt Elezene,' I'd say. I talked about how I was going to miss him and how happy I'd been to have him live close to me in his last years. I did try to avoid speeding, as I didn't want any questions about what I was doing. It's legal to transport bodies across state lines as long as they're embalmed, but I didn't want to have to explain that to a police officer."

Though there were some tears at several points along the journey, it wasn't a sad trip. "It was a chance to relive a lot of memories," she said. "The most emotional moment came when we crossed the North Carolina line, which meant that Dad was home again. I hadn't expected that to move me so, but it did."

Once they arrived in West Jefferson, her father's body was put into a more dignified receptacle, a traditional coffin. Most of those gathered at his funeral had no idea of how he'd been transported to his final resting place.

Looking back, Marian views their ride from Mississippi to North Carolina as the last gift she gave her father. "I think it was a comfort to him to know that at the end of his life, he'd be taken home by me," she said. "He'd taken care of me my entire life, and now it was my turn."

My friend Elizabeth, an Episcopal priest, was apologetic. "I can't do the graveside committal after Roger's funeral service," she said. "Would you be able do it? You'd need to ride in the hearse to the cemetery too—are you OK with that?"

Well, actually I am. Thank you for asking, in fact.

And so a few days later, there I was, riding shotgun in a hearse with my deceased friend Roger behind me, thinking of Marian and her last ride with her dad.

I'd known Roger for two decades. He'd served on my discernment committee when I was considering becoming a deacon. He was kind and wise, the sort of man people depended upon for whatever needed doing in the church. As his health failed, it saddened me to see his gradual slipping away. One Sunday at church he sat down beside me and asked me a question that I sensed had been on his mind for some time.

"Will you speak at my funeral?"

"Of course," I said. "But don't rush it."

A few months later, I stood at a podium and fulfilled my promise, summing up his life of love and integrity in a few hundred words. As I got into the hearse, I patted the glass that separated the front from the back, where the casket was topped with an elaborate flower arrangement.

"It's good to be here with you, Roger," I said.

The forty-five-minute drive passed surprisingly quickly. The funeral director was happy to have company, especially someone genuinely interested in his work. He'd grown up in the business, he told me, and his parents were always on call when he was growing up. His dad continues to take the hardest cases—the suicides and deaths of young people, especially.

When we arrived at the cemetery, I watched as the casket was taken out of the hearse and carried by Roger's sons and grandsons to the grave site, a ritual that's been repeated for millennia. Our parents carried us, and at the end of their lives, it's our turn to carry them. Whether their remains are in an urn or a casket, riding in the back of our van or in a funeral hearse, the weight of them is heavy indeed.

Watching the procession, I wondered how long it would be before I'd be standing at the grave of my mother.

A statue of St. Francis near San Damiano Church in Assisi
(PHOTO CREDIT: BOB SESSIONS)

9

Welcoming Sister Death

Rome and Assisi

"Skip the line?" A freelance guide in St. Peter's Square at the Vatican was eager to make a sale to a couple of confused-looking tourists. "Thirty dollars and you won't have to wait to get into the basilica."

Seeing the line of hundreds of people that wound across the huge square, Bob and I were tempted. Though we knew admission to the church was free, it looked like it would take at least an hour to wind our way to its entrance.

"We already have tickets to the Necropolis," I said. "Do we have to wait in line anyway?"

"Thirty dollars and you won't have to wait," the guide repeated.

Another guide stepped up, giving the man a disapproving look. "Just go to the side entrance," she said, pointing to the left of the basilica. "Those tickets will get you in without waiting."

Feeling grateful, we headed across the square. In my hand I clutched the precious tickets I'd ordered six months before. Limited to about 250 people a day, the tour of the Necropolis is one of the hardest-to-score tickets in Rome. The Scavi—an Italian word meaning excavations—is the archaeological site underneath the basilica, the place where the remains of the apostle Peter are said to lie. When Jesus said that Peter was the rock upon which the church would be built, the Catholics took him literally: St. Peter's Basilica is built over St. Peter's bones.

Touring an underground graveyard was a peculiar way to spend a sunny afternoon in a capital renowned for its beauty, but I hoped that this city of the dead (the English translation of the Greek word *nekropolis*) would help me better understand the Eternal City that lies above it. I was curious, too, why my ecclesiastical cousins the Roman Catholics had preserved this ancient site underneath their most magnificent church. My own branch of Christianity doesn't do much with relics, but my fondness for the more esoteric parts of religious belief put the Necropolis at the top of my Rome agenda.

As we walked across St. Peter's Square, I felt a sense of déjà vu. Thanks to movies and TV, the massive baroque facade of the basilica and the long colonnades extending on either side seemed familiar. And in the plaza's center was a landmark that made me recall my travels in Egypt: an eighty-two-foot obelisk that was erected in 37 CE during the time when this spot was a Roman circus, an open-air venue used for public entertainments such as chariot races and executions. The cross on its top looked distinctly like an add-on.

Passing through security, we entered a much quieter area filled with buildings housing Vatican bureaucrats. A helpful Swiss Guard—dressed in the photogenic, though slightly ludicrous, outfit of his tribe—directed us to a small ticket booth a short distance away. There we joined a group of ten Americans who had also signed up for a tour of the Necropolis led by a seminarian from the Pontifical North American College in Rome. After struggling to make our way in the city with no Italian other than *buongiorno* and *gelato, per favore*, I heard the young man's accent with relief.

Introducing himself as Justin, he welcomed us to the tour. "You're going to see a part of the Vatican most people don't know much about," he said.

He began by leading us just a few steps away to a marker we'd walked over without noticing: a small plaque embedded in the paving stones. Justin explained that before the construction of the new St. Peter's Basilica, the obelisk now on the square had stood here.

"Tradition says that the apostle Peter was martyred next to the obelisk," Justin said. "He asked to be crucified upside down, because he felt he wasn't worthy to be killed in the same way as his master."

I was pleased to be reminded of the man for whom the basilica was named, a fisherman who'd been poor his entire life, because my entry into the Vatican had made me feel a bit Martin Luther-ish. In 1510, the German monk's reactions to what he saw in Rome helped spark the Protestant Reformation. I wasn't ready to go as far as Luther, but the whole place did seem a little over the top, even for someone with a high tolerance for high church. But here, in this quiet corner of the Vatican, a grittier spiritual history was commemorated. I was eager to learn more.

After leading us through a side entrance into the basilica, Justin continued his story. Following Peter's death on the cross, he said, his followers removed the body and buried it nearby in a simple earthen grave. Its location was passed down from generation to generation of believers. About fifty years after his death, the area around the emperor Nero's circus became a place for other burials. In ancient Rome, it was illegal to bury people inside the city walls, and so tombs were often located next to the roads leading into the city (the hope was that the dead would be remembered by the living as they passed by).

"Then at the beginning of the fourth century, after Christianity was no longer outlawed, the emperor Constantine began building a church over the remains of St. Peter," said Justin. "The people of Rome were asked to remove their dead from the tombs. The area was filled with earth and the first St. Peter's Basilica was constructed on top. It wasn't until 1939 that excavations began on the Roman-era necropolis."

By this time we'd made our way down a set of stairs and into the bowels of the basilica, where we entered a narrow corridor bordered by two rows of side-by-side, small buildings. Constructed of brick, the tombs looked like miniature houses, with windows and doorways that allowed us to peer inside. As we passed them, Justin pointed out details that reflected the lives of those once interred within. One had an image of the falcon-headed Egyptian god Horus on its wall; others featured mosaics and frescoes showing scenes from Roman mythology. Most had niches embedded in their walls for remains, and over their doorways were Latin inscriptions giving information about the dead, from freedmen who'd become wealthy merchants to aristocratic families boasting of their lineage.

At last we came to our destination: the place where Peter's remains are kept in a clear box tucked into a crevice in the rock wall. All that was visible was a small glimpse of bones.

"We can't know for certain that these are the remains of St. Peter," Justin said, answering our unspoken question. "But ancient sources say that St. Peter was buried in this area, and DNA evidence indicates that the bones are from a man between the ages of sixty and seventy. And they're wrapped in a purple cloth, suggesting they were highly valued. But in the end, people have to make up their own minds."

Saying that he would leave us for private prayer, he exited the room. While most of the group filed out after him, several of us stayed. Instead of praying, I thought of the huge weight of the basilica above us, remembering my time inside the Great Pyramids at Giza. Like those immense edifices, all of the Vatican's magnificence is built upon a graveyard.

WHERE THE DEAD KEEP WATCH

I'd wanted to visit Rome ever since I was a child, when I devoured stories of its gods, goddesses, emperors, and generals. When I finally visited the city in person, its vitality exhilarated me—the sidewalk cafés filled with people late into the night, the tiny shops crowded with customers buying artisan cheeses and meats, the motorbikes and taxis zipping by on its streets. More than any other city I've visited, Rome pulsed with life.

And yet, I encountered the dead almost everywhere I went. In museums, the marble heads of noblemen stared at me with impassive eyes. At the Coliseum, where free entertainments once included fights with wild animals in the morning, public executions at midday, and gladiator contests in the evening, I learned that an estimated half-million people had been killed on its stage. On the Appian Way, the ancient Roman highway that led from the port city of Brindisi to the Roman Forum, tombs lined the route, many bearing the carved stone faces of their inhabitants. Through the millennia they'd seen many people pass by, from slaves and merchants to centurions and emperors. They looked unimpressed by the current crop of bicyclists and joggers wearing brightly colored athletic wear instead of togas.

In Rome's churches, martyrs were ubiquitous, often portrayed with the instruments of their demise: there was Stephen holding the rocks that had been used to stone him, and Sebastian posing with an arrow. I saw a marble St. Cecelia lying underneath an altar with her throat cut, looking appropriately pale, given the blood she'd lost. And nearly every altar, of course, had Jesus hanging limp upon his cross.

I remembered that in Mexico, my guide had speculated that the residents of Teotihuacán abandoned their magnificent city after it was attacked, believing that because it had been born it was destined to die as well. The Romans, in contrast, refused to take destruction as a final answer, rebuilding again and again through the centuries.

After barbarians from the north captured Rome in the fifth century (full disclosure: my ancestors were among them), the city shrank to a fraction of its former size. In subsequent centuries, it was the once-persecuted Christians, ironically, who brought it back to life. Churches were built over pagan temples, and the Vatican became the center of a religious and political web. During the Renaissance, popes invited the greatest artists of the age to decorate their churches, with Michelangelo and other luminaries adorning them with ever-greater splendor.

But just as the Vatican is constructed over the bones of Peter, Rome stands upon a pagan foundation. Walking down a busy street, we often came upon archaeological sites, their broken-down columns and walls surrounded by modern shops and flats. The ruins reminded me of the elderly people in wheelchairs who line the hallways in many nursing homes, mutely evoking the past.

Though most cities lack Rome's rich history, even a brand-new suburb is built upon death, of course. The trees and plants that once flourished upon its land were destroyed by developers, and the soil itself is the result of millennia of decay. Even the energy that lights our homes and powers our vehicles comes from plants that died eons ago. If we just look around, we have good evidence that everything dies and is reborn as something else.

I'm tempted to speculate that Rome is so comfortable with death because it's steeped in Christianity, a religion that emphasizes resurrection. But the Romans have followed other religions in their history, and many of these faiths also have a belief in an afterlife. In San Clemente Church near the Coliseum, for example, we descended through several layers of archaeological excavations until at last we stood beside a Mithraeum, a place where the Roman god Mithras was worshiped. As I looked into the dimly lit room with its rock walls and stone benches, I imagined the mystery rites that once took place here. In its center was a post bearing the image of a man sacrificing a bull—a pagan echo of the crucified Jesus who hangs upon a cross several layers above, at the altar where the priests celebrate mass.

If Rome is indeed the Eternal City, perhaps it's because its residents figured out a long time ago how to live comfortably with death. Through its art, its ruins, and its churches, the city continually reminds its citizens that they're mortal. You might be remembered for a while, or you might not. But while you're alive, enjoy la dolce vita, the sweet life. Savor the warmth of the sun on your face. Have another bite of gelato. It won't last, and neither will you.

The name of what's popularly known as Rome's Protestant Cemetery is a misnomer, a guide told me at its gate.

"We have Catholics here—mostly people who wanted to be buried next to their non-Catholic relatives," he said. "And we have members of other religions too."

No matter what their faith, the dead in this graveyard are a who's who of mostly foreign-born artists, authors, and political leaders, people who had fallen under the spell of the city and didn't want to leave it, even in death. Many came from northern Europe, fleeing the overcast skies, mediocre food, and repressed citizens of their home countries. One meal of *bucatini all'amatriciana* and an afternoon spent lounging in the sunlight of the Piazza Navona meant that they could never go home again.

We toured the cemetery on our last day in Rome, bookending our stay in the city with graveyards. Unlike the claustrophobic environs of the Necropolis underneath St. Peter's, this sun-dappled cemetery invited lingering. Bordered by walls that muffle the sounds of the city and filled with well-tended flowers, bushes, and trees, it's a showcase for funereal art. In one section, an angel drapes herself over a coffin in grief. In another, a young man reclines on his side atop his tomb, his faithful lapdog tucked into a curve of his arm. Nearby a boy perches on a small pillar, his head turned to watch visitors approach. At its entrance there's even a pyramid, constructed in the first century CE by a merchant who'd caught the bug for all things Egyptian.

This cemetery's most famous inhabitants are the nineteenth-century poets Percy Bysshe Shelley and John Keats. In what turned out to be a stroke of luck for their posthumous literary careers, both had tragic, early deaths. Keats, who had come to Rome to soak up its warmth and sunlight in a vain effort to treat his tuberculosis, died at twenty-five. Shelley drowned off the coast of Italy at twenty-nine years of age (in his pocket was found a book of Keats's poems). Their deaths set a high bar for their fellow Romantic Era poets.

Like many writers, I sometimes amuse myself by composing my epitaph—one last chance to impress readers with my words. I've long envied the ones chosen by Keats before his death, a sentence brilliant in its brevity and power: "Here lies One Whose Name was writ in Water." But until I stood at his grave I hadn't appreciated the full poignancy of this statement. Keats, whose work received such scathing reviews that they were said to have contributed to his death, was certain that nothing he wrote would be remembered.

Yet today the people who visit his grave, especially the English majors like myself who've memorized "Ode on a Grecian Urn," look at that epitaph and sigh. It's a pleasant sigh, in keeping with the enjoyable melancholy of the Romantic Era, but still, it's full of regret. If only Keats had known how his literary standing would improve after he'd breathed his last.

Standing by his grave, I thought of all the ways people try to ensure that they'll be remembered, from long epitaphs and grand mausoleums to commissioned portraits. I had read many markers with variations of "Never Forgotten," a statement made with the best of intentions but nearly always thwarted by the passage of time. Keats teaches us that earthly immortality isn't something we can orchestrate. Even if we place our tombs next to busy thoroughfares and have our likeness sculpted in marble, the odds are good that we'll be forgotten. 'Tis best to let time sort out who gets remembered and who doesn't.

When Oscar Wilde—ever a fan of extravagant gestures— visited this cemetery in 1877, he prostrated himself at Keats's grave, calling it "the holiest place in Rome." Forget the pagan temples, the Vatican, and the many churches in the city— instead he found the sacred here, at the grave of a young man he'd met only through his words, which turned out to be immortal after all.

GOD'S FOOL

In the Italian countryside, a man was dying. Though he'd been born into wealth, he'd lived in poverty for decades. Illness had reduced his body to a near skeleton, and he was blind from an eye condition that had plagued him for years. He spent his last days in terrible pain.

But Francesco (a nickname meaning something like "Frenchie") Bernardone was not an ordinary beggar. His lack of material resources was self-imposed. He was surrounded by people who loved him. And when he died in 1226 at the age of forty-four, he was almost immediately declared a saint. We know him as St. Francis, the beloved patron saint of animals and the environment, and the brown-robed, genial overseer of gardens.

Bob and I arrived in his hometown of Assisi after a week in Rome, thankful for our time there but also relieved to leave its noise and crowds for a quieter destination. A two-hour train trip took us through the pastoral countryside of Umbria to the base of a hill town that looked like a medieval painting, its picturesque stone buildings silhouetted against a blue sky. As we exited the train, I noticed another passenger who'd just disembarked, a man who was standing motionless on the platform, his eyes drinking in the vista above. Seeing his joyful face, I sensed that he was praying, and that his journey to Assisi had taken him a long time, much longer than a two-hour train ride from Rome.

If things had gone according to his father's plan, Francis would have grown up to inherit the family business of dealing in imported, luxurious fabrics. But as he entered adulthood he spent more and more time carousing instead of working. Handsome, charismatic, and spendthrift, he hosted so many feasts and revels that his friends dubbed him King of the Parties.

When a militia was formed to fight against the neighboring town of Perugia, Francis signed up, eager to add some knightly glory to his reputation. In the battle he was wounded and taken captive, then confined in an underground vault where he languished for almost a year, plagued by the malaria and tuberculosis that would afflict him for the rest of his life. When he returned to Assisi, his former pastimes held little appeal to him, and he struggled to adapt. He decided that more military service was the answer to his ennui and left to join the Crusades, but just twenty-two miles from Assisi he heard a voice telling him to return home (though it might have been the malaria talking instead of God).

Back home, Francesco continued to languish. One day he found himself drawn to the dilapidated church of San Damiano, where no one had worshiped for years. A cross hung above its altar, a crucified Christ who seemed to gaze directly at him. As Francis prayed, he heard a voice saying to him from this cross, "Francis, go rebuild my house." Proving once again that God really does need to be clearer in his messages—a perennial problem throughout history—Francis thought he was supposed to rebuild San Damiano. It was only later that he figured out that God was talking Church with a capital C.

When Francis took bolts of cloth from his father's shop and sold them to raise funds for the renovation of San Damiano, his angry father first thrashed him, then locked him in a room. His mother let him out several weeks later, but the two soon clashed again when his father demanded the funds from the sale of the cloth. Francis (who probably should be the patron saint of rebellious teenagers as well as animals) gave his response in dramatic fashion. In the middle of Assisi he stripped off his clothes and left them and a purse of money at his father's feet. From now on, he announced, he would have only one father: his Father in heaven.

For the rest of his life, Francis wore a rough tunic instead of the expensive fabrics of his youth, an outward symbol of his inner transformation. He became as extravagant in his piety as he'd once been in his partying, stripping everything from his life that didn't draw him closer to God. He served the poor with tenderness and love, especially the lepers who endured a miserable existence on the outskirts of Assisi society. He became a mentor to many, including a young noblewoman named Clare who founded a religious order known as the Poor Clares. And he deeply loved the natural world, drawing inspiration from its beauties and forming friendships with fellow creatures ranging from crickets to a wolf that was ravaging a nearby town (after a talk with Francis, the wolf agreed to stop).

During an era when much of the church was plagued by scandal, corruption, and greed, Francis was an evangelist for voluntary poverty, service to the marginalized, love for nature, and a transcendent, joyful love of God. His radical alternative to the spiritual status quo caused his fame to spread throughout Europe. His critics called him God's Fool, a name that he likely didn't mind at all.

Assisi looks like a medieval village that's been dipped into a bucket and scrubbed clean. Constructed on a steep hill, its narrow lanes wind between impossibly quaint stone buildings, their balconies and steps filled with blooming flowers. Even the tourist shops are charming, their shelves filled with miniature St. Francises and St. Clares extending their hands in blessing.

Appropriately, our stay in Assisi coincided with All Saints' Day, the Christian holiday that technically honors the saints but in practice includes all the dead, regardless of their sanctity. Italy, like many Catholic countries, observes November 1 as a national holiday. In Assisi we discovered they were also celebrating an equally sacred event: the olive harvest. The town's central piazza, the same one where tradition says Francis renounced his father, had tents where farmers and artisans sold freshly pressed oil and locally made cheeses, meats, and breads. The scene brought to mind my favorite Italian saying: "At the table, one never grows old." As I savored a piece of thick-crusted peasant bread dipped into an aromatic oil, I wondered if this is the true secret of immortality.

The double holiday had brought many visitors to the town, from couples and families enjoying a long weekend to brown-robed men and women whose clothing marked them as members of the Franciscan order. Many hailed from countries far away, showing the global reach of the movement founded by Francis.

Throughout the day, masses were held in the town's half-dozen churches, each service announced by the tolling of bells. The chimes made me think of the Mexicans half a world away who were celebrating Día de los Muertos, arranging photos, foods, and mementos on *ofrendas* and making plans to go to the cemeteries that night. A year had passed since I'd visited the Day of the Dead celebration in Chicago. It felt fitting to be in Assisi on this day, listening to the bells. By now I knew exactly for whom those bells tolled: they tolled for me.

It was John Donne who coined the famous phrase, one that Ernest Hemingway used as the title of a novel about the Spanish Civil War. Donne, who lived during the early seventeenth century, was intimately acquainted with death from both personal experience and his work as an Anglican priest. One day in 1623, as he suffered from a fever that he feared might kill him, he heard a church bell tolling at a funeral and wrote these words:

> No man is an island, entire of itself; every man is a piece of the continent, a part of the main. If a clod be washed away by the sea, Europe is the less, as well as if a promontory were, as well as if a manor of thy friend's, or of thine own were: any man's death diminishes me, because I am involved in mankind, and therefore never send to know for whom the bell tolls; it tolls for thee.

I stood in the piazza in Assisi, thinking of Francis, who wore his life as lightly as the cloak he flung at his father's feet, and of all the dead I'd encountered in my travels. I was beginning to realize the kinship I shared with them, these people from whom I was separated only by the steady in-and-out of my breathing.

Like countless pilgrims before us, we followed the footsteps of Francis through Assisi. We started at San Damiano, the church where Francis received his famous message from the cross. Now it's as pristine and tidy as the town, a stone structure that became the first monastery of the Order of the Poor Clares in 1216.

San Damiano is the site of another important event in the life of Francis: it is here that he composed the Canticle of the Creatures, a song that's thought to be among the first works of literature in Italian. Each verse is addressed to those whom Francis considered part of his family, from Brother Sun and Sister Moon to Brother Wind and Sister Water. This song, a litany of wonder for the ways nature reflects the glory of God, has done much to cement Francis's reputation as a free-spirited hippie, though in reality he was a far more complex man, not easily categorized as either liberal or conservative, traditional or iconoclastic.

The Basilica of St. Francis dominates Assisi both visually and spiritually. Located on a promontory just below the town, its two levels contain glorious works of art by Renaissance masters, making this a pilgrimage site for artists as well as spiritual seekers. While the grandeur of the church seemed at odds with the humble life of its namesake, I couldn't help but marvel at the artwork within, especially the frescoes by Giotto showing scenes from the life of Francis. The most famous one depicts him preaching to a flock of birds, another piece of evidence that Francis wasn't your typical man of God. The birds look curious, but not entirely convinced.

A steep walk up Mount Subasio took us to a place that seemed much more in keeping with the spirit of Francis: the Eremo delle Carceri, a hermitage tucked into a wooded gorge overlooking Assisi, a place where he and his followers often retreated to pray. Just outside the building is a statue of Francis that's the happiest depiction of a saint I've ever seen. It shows him lying on the ground, his hands behind his head, his sandals kicked off and ankles crossed, a contented smile on his face. Christianity might produce more saints if we pictured them like this, rather than carrying the tools of their martyrdom.

In the valley below Assisi we next toured the Basilica of St. Mary of the Angels, the motherhouse for the Franciscan order. It's actually a church within a church, because in its center stands the small, one-room Porziuncola (meaning "little portion"). This is one of three chapels that Francis restored before he understood that God wanted him to restore all of Christianity, not just a few buildings. Near it he built a small hut, and soon he was joined by a small band of followers attracted to his revolutionary teachings. He named them the Friars Minor, the little brothers, as a reminder that they were always to remain humble.

As Francis neared the end of his life, blind and ailing, he was brought here. He apologized to his body—Brother Donkey, as he referred to it—because he'd treated it too harshly during his life. Then he asked a favor of those gathered around him: when it came time for him to die, he wanted them to place his naked body on the ground, not long, just about the length of time it took someone to walk a mile, he said.

Such an odd request, I thought as I stood before the altar near the Porziuncola marking the place where Francis died. Perhaps it was symbolically linked to his dramatic gesture in the piazza when he claimed God as his only father. Or maybe he knew that after his death his bones—and his message—would become the property of the church, which would inevitably try to corral and domesticate the wild spirit he'd unleashed. Before that happened, he would have one last moment of communion with the earth he loved so much.

It is said that when Francis died, a chorus of larks wheeled and swooped above him for a long time, singing him home.

Before I left Assisi, I returned one last time to the Basilica of St. Francis. This time I wanted to visit the church's small museum, which displays some of the treasures donated to the shrine through the centuries, from ornate tapestries to gleaming silver altarpieces. The man who sat at its entrance was eager to talk, making me suspect that the museum attracted far fewer visitors than the church. As we chatted, I learned that he was a lay Franciscan, someone who'd moved to Assisi from the United States.

"Is it as peaceful here as it seems?" I asked.

"I think part of the reason why Assisi has a reputation for serenity is that most people arrive here after spending time in Rome," he said, smiling. "Any place is going to seem quiet after that."

But then he admitted that Assisi does have a peaceful atmosphere, perhaps nurtured by all the people who've come here on pilgrimage through the centuries. "Maybe their prayers have seeped into this place," he said.

I told him that I was visiting on All Saints' Day as part of my quest to come to terms with mortality and asked what he thought Francis has to teach us about death.

He seemed intrigued by the question, taking his time to answer. When he spoke again, he talked about how ever-present death was during Francis's day, coming in the form of infections, accidents, wars, and illnesses of many kinds. Religious faith provided a refuge, but people were also fearful about what would happen to them after they died. Remembering the many depictions of judgment day in the churches of Rome, which were full of tormented souls plummeting into hell pursued by demons, I could see why they were worried.

"You've been to the Porziuncola?" he asked. "That's where his life ended, you know. And just before he died, he called his friends to him and had them write down a final stanza to his famous song, the one about Brother Sun and Sister Moon. In it he praises Sister Death, welcoming her just as he'd welcomed all the other forces of nature into his life."

His words brought to mind the hymn "All Creatures of Our God and King," which is based on the Canticle of the Creatures. I remembered the verse about death:

> And even you, most gentle death,
> waiting to hush our final breath,
> O praise him, Alleluia!
> You lead back home the child of God,
> for Christ our Lord that way has trod:
> O praise him, O praise him,
> Alleluia, alleluia, alleluia!

I'd sung those alleluias many times, including at the funerals of people I dearly loved. But I never knew that Francis had originally referred to death as *sister*, which gave those alleluias a deeper layer of meaning. No Grim Reaper for Francis: like the sun, moon, wind, and water, death was kin to him. And his choice to view death as feminine seemed significant as well. Perhaps he thought that since a woman had given him life, another woman would take it away.

Thanking the guide for his time, I made my way back to the lower level of the basilica, thinking some more about Francis's words. That sibling relationship could play itself out in many ways, I realized. You might have a nurturing sister who's unfailingly supportive and kind, or one who calls you hysterically in the middle of the night begging for a loan to pay her casino debts. She might live half a continent away or in the house down the street, be happily married or on her fifteenth loser boyfriend. The relationships range from wildly dysfunctional to affectionate, and there's not one right way of relating to her. But she's a presence in our lives, whether we acknowledge her or not. Like death.

Inside the church, I came upon an image I remembered from my earlier tour, one that I wanted to ponder again. The fresco, which adorns a wall near the main altar, shows a brown-robed Francis standing next to a skeleton. I gazed upward at the figures for a long time. I could see how the two were perfectly at ease with each other. The figure of Death is wearing rags but also has a gold crown on its head, slightly askew. Francis is holding up one hand that shows the stigmata, the mark of crucifixion that he miraculously received as a sign of his devotion to his master, a man who taught him that death is not the end. And his other hand rests lightly on the skeleton's shoulder. Have no fear, Francis seems to be saying. Death is part of the family.

Sacred Stone Circle at Harvest Preserve in Iowa City
(PHOTO CREDIT: BOB SESSIONS)

Epilogue
At the Stones

In the nursing home, my mother continues to slip away. At each visit I see an incremental decline: her body is a little smaller, her eyes more detached, her conversation more elliptical.

But still, her essence remains, and she has a kindness now that wasn't always as visible earlier in her life. The dementia wheel of fortune often brings anger, anxiety, and fear, but sometimes, as with my mother, it delivers sweetness. I realize that this has been the basis of her character all along—a welcome reminder when I remember the difficulties of our relationship in earlier years. This stage will not last, and much harder times likely lie ahead, but while it does, I welcome it.

She still enjoys life too. On her eighty-eighth birthday, for example, she was delighted that her name was kept up on the bulletin board for two days. "Happy birthday, Grace!" it said. She pointed out the words to me over and over when I visited her.

"I'm the only person who's had their birthday up on the board for two days," she said. "To think that I've become popular at my age!"

I agreed that it's a remarkable thing.

I've gotten better at simply being with her. This is the new normal for us, and there are undeniable benefits. She often tells me how happy she is, and it touches me to see how the staff genuinely cares for her. She seems more comfortable and at ease with herself than ever before. Ironically, dementia has unlocked some of the best parts of her character.

On one visit, the yellow barrier that she'd once insisted upon having at her door, the one saying "Stop" to visitors, is gone. When I ask her about it, she doesn't remember she ever used it to keep people out. She still keeps a chair pushed against the door from the inside, but her defenses are less fierce now on every front. She spends much of her time in the communal living area, helping the staff with small tasks and occasionally chiding the other residents for not working hard enough. The criticism, of course, doesn't register with them, but I think my mom likes the fact that she's still doing her part to keep the world going.

Over a glass of wine with Allyson, the angel reader who's now become a friend, she asked me a question out of the blue. "Your brother is here," she said. "He wants to ask you something. He wants to know if it's OK for him to call your mom home."

It took me only the briefest of moments to realize the significance of her words. My dead brother is not talking about a phone call. I blinked back tears. "Of course," I replied.

And it *is* all right. Her death might come next week, or next month, or in a year or two or three, but whenever she dies, I will wish her Godspeed to whatever comes next and give thanks for her life on this earth. She's been a wonderful mother and grandmother. She's known love and happiness and done her best to improve her small corner of existence. I believe that when she dies, she'll be welcomed by her husband, son, and other family members, including her beloved father, who died before I was born. I like to think of the party in heaven awaiting her, when she wakes up on the other side, the fog cleared from her mind at last.

And on the next All Saints' Day, I will add her photo to my Day of the Dead altar.

Nearly every week I visit the place where my ashes are likely to be scattered. Barring some unexpected circumstance, my earthly remains will mingle with the earth at Harvest Preserve, a nondenominational spiritual center near my home in Iowa.

The sanctuary exists because a set of prehistoric standing stones in Indonesia wanted to come to Iowa (go ahead, read that sentence again). The preserve's founder, an eccentric philanthropist named Doug Paul, heard about the stones from an antiquities dealer in the late 1990s. Little was known of their origin, except that they were quarried with stone chisels at least four thousand years ago and were at one time arranged in a circle on the island of Flores. Wanting to get rid of them because they were too pagan, the residents of the island planned to push them into the sea. Instead, Doug bought them and arranged for the basalt stones, each weighing between three thousand and twenty thousand pounds, to be brought to Iowa by ship, train, and flatbed truck, a process that took more than a year. When they arrived, he had them erected on property he and his wife, Linda, had purchased on the edge of town, farmland that the city was planning to turn into housing developments.

"The stones were sending me a message from across the world," Doug told me. "For whatever reason, they wanted to be here in Iowa. From the very beginning of this effort, I felt like I was put on a need-to-know basis. At each step I found out what I needed to know to go forward, but I didn't get all the answers I wanted. I still don't have them. I'm a pretty unlikely person to make this happen, but it felt like something I was called to do."

Having heard a number of inexplicable calls in my own life, I thought that his words made surprising sense.

Today Harvest Preserve protects one hundred acres of prairie and woods, all managed by a nonprofit foundation that will ensure its existence for generations to come. Doug devotes much of his time to maintaining the property, gradually bringing back more of its native flora and fauna. "I used to own the land, and now it owns me," is the way he describes his role there.

When I first visited Harvest Preserve four years ago, it took me about a minute to decide I wanted to become a member. In the years since, my bond to this place has deepened. I love its trails that wind beneath oaks and maples and its ever-changing vistas of sky and prairie. But most of all, I love the Sacred Stone Circle that sits in a meadow overlooking the woods. The stones from Indonesia, planted deep in Iowa soil, look completely at home.

I visit these stones at least once a week when I'm not traveling. On summer mornings, I often have coffee among them, sitting at the base of one that gives me a good view of the prairie that surrounds the circle. At some point in the future, I'd like my ashes to be scattered right where my eyes rest as I'm sipping my morning brew. It pleases me to think of spending eternity there, my ashes slowly being absorbed by the waving grasses of the meadow. And I love the fact that I'll be near the Indonesian stones, these tall friends who share my love both for travel and for Iowa.

Our species has had many thousands of years to ponder death, and the chances are slim that anyone, including me, can say something about mortality that hasn't already been pondered countless times before.

That said, I think each of us needs to find our own way through the thicket of speculation about our eventual deaths and what comes next, if anything. I like Doug's observation that at each step we're given what we need to go forward but not all the answers we want. This makes surrender an essential part of the entire process, an acknowledgment of our powerlessness in the face of mystery. The older I get, the more I see this need for surrender as a gift and not a curse.

My trips have given me valuable insights, and I give thanks for what the Egyptians, Maori, Mexicans, Crestonians, and

Italians have taught me about death. My budding meditation practice helps me too. Gradually, ever so slowly, I'm settling into a practice that I hope to continue for the rest of my life. I've had no great insights, no grand visions. But that sinking into tranquility, even for just a few moments at a time, happens more easily for me now. One. Two. Three. Four. I count my breaths, knowing they're numbered.

Throughout the writing of this book, Doug Paul has been preparing another sacred site at Harvest Preserve, one where people can hold services for their loved ones and then scatter their ashes somewhere on the property.

I've watched the construction process with great interest—first the clearing and leveling of the site, then the building of a platform and the installation of a tall limestone pillar in its center. When the project is complete, about forty Indonesian standing stones will surround the pillar (surprise, surprise—when the Indonesians heard that Doug was interested in old pagan stones, they found some more they could part with).

The shrine faces west into the setting sun and overlooks a wide expanse of prairie and woods. The twelve-foot monument in its center has the symbols of the seven chakras on one side, while its other side bears a bronze plaque with these words:

> When on that single thought
>   of love I fix my sight,
> And waves of bliss drown
>   every earth delight,
> I leave my place and rise
>   in heavenly flight,
> On soft, unfolding wings
>   of Holy Light.

"The words came to me one night years ago," Doug told me. "I thought I'd put them on my own grave marker, but then I realized that they're actually meant for this spot."

As I walk the trails of the preserve, I sometimes think of the service that will likely be held here for me at some point in the future. It's sad to contemplate leaving my loved ones, and I'm sorry for the pain they'll feel at my death. Another regret, one that's much smaller but still present, is that I won't be able to write about my trip to the afterlife, the most remarkable journey of them all.

But then I look at the inscription on the limestone pillar. I like the expansiveness of its words, which to me convey a hint of the ineffable. Eventually I will rise in heavenly flight into the light. But not yet. Not yet. And today is a good day to walk this earth.

Acknowledgments

I'm grateful to all the people who thought writing a book about travel and death wasn't a crazy idea, especially those who shared with me their personal reflections and stories about mortality. In particular, my conversations with Allyson Schulte, Marian Wingo, William Blair, Jody Hovland, Lisa Bormann, Scott Temple, Wendelin Guentner, Susan Lutgendorf, Andrea Billhardt, Teri Breitbach, Darcy Lipsius, Rebecca Christian Patience, Jane Dohrmann, Elizabeth Coulter, Virginia Houser, Janet Freeman, Deborah Logan, and Dan Ciha added greatly to my understanding and knowledge.

Loren Horton tutored me with good humor and comprehensive expertise about death and mourning customs. Barb Lewis proved to me once again that a friend who's also a skilled editor is a great asset. Scott Samuelson and Sarah Kyle told me just where I needed to go in Rome, and Lindy Weilgart invited me to Vienna and then didn't complain when I said I wanted to visit a cemetery and funeral museum.

Helen Tomei, founder and president of Sacred Earth Journeys, has helped many travelers explore holy sites around the world with sensitivity and respect, including me. I'm grateful as well to Miguel Angel for his wisdom and kindness, and to Brian Witzke, who is a wonderful companion for exploring almost anything, including Mayan temples.

In Crestone, Kairina Danforth, Christian Dillo, John Milton, and David Scott provided a warm welcome and keen insights into their unique community and its diverse faith traditions.

In New Zealand, I'm grateful to Hone Mihaka of Taiamai Tours in the Bay of Islands and to the staff of TIME Unlimited

Tours in Auckland, especially Te Kaahu Ripo O Ngaa Rangi Tuitui and Ceillhe Sperath.

Honoring Your Wishes is one of a growing number of programs that encourage people to do advance health care planning so that if they can't communicate because of ill health, their loved ones will know their medical preferences. Because of the work being done through programs like this one, the American way of death is slowly changing for the better. If you haven't had a conversation yet with your loved ones about end-of-life issues, I hope this book might convince you to do so. I consider my advance health care directive one of the best gifts I've ever given my family.

I'm grateful to the staff of the Aase Haugen Home in Decorah, Iowa, for giving compassionate and loving care to both my father and mother, and to my sister, Julie Fahlin, for being a steady source of support and kindness.

Greg Daniel, my agent, and Jessica Miller Kelley, my editor at Westminster John Knox Press, provided invaluable assistance in making this book a reality.

I'm thankful to Doug and Linda Paul and Julie Decker for the creation and ongoing maintenance of Harvest Preserve, a place from which I draw great spiritual sustenance. And to the good people of New Song Episcopal Church: thanks for always welcoming me back, no matter how long I've been gone.

Most of all, I'm grateful for my family's abiding love and enthusiastic cheerleading for whatever project I undertake. My husband, Bob Sessions, is the best conversation partner and traveling companion imaginable, closely followed by our sons, Owen and Carl Sessions. Thanks to all of you for being willing to talk about anything, including death, and for always being up for an adventure.

This book is dedicated with love to my parents, brother, and grandfather: Myron, Grace, Alan, and Carl Erickson. When I cross the Jordan, I hope to meet all of you again on the other side.

Discussion Questions

1. Have you ever visited a place that made you think about mortality? If so, what about it made you reflect on issues of life and death?

2. Which of Erickson's journeys did you find most thought-provoking? Why?

3. What events in your life have forced you to confront your own mortality?

4. Erickson quotes author Richard Rohr as saying you don't want to leave your spiritual homework until the night before the test. For you, what might that spiritual homework include?

5. Who in your life has been a role model for how to die well? What made their death a good death?

6. Are you afraid of dying? Why or why not?

7. What do you think happens after we die?

8. Erickson writes, "While a terminal diagnosis frequently jolts people into contemplating spiritual questions, aging often happens so slowly that we can easily miss the chance to learn from it" (34). Do you think this is true? If so, what are the spiritual lessons to be learned from aging?

9. Has your perspective on mortality changed as you've grown older?

10. What rituals or practices do you think would help people in our society better deal with mortality? Have you learned anything from this book that you'd like to incorporate in your own life?

11. Erickson describes some of the beliefs relating to ancestors in cultures across the globe. Have you ever felt that you've received a message from someone who has died?

12. Does the Mexican Day of the Dead holiday appeal to you in any way? Why or why not?

13. How can faith communities better support and care for people at the end of their lives?

14. Have you ever tried to meditate? Do you think meditation can be a tool for dealing with aging and preparing for death?

15. Do you have an advance health care directive? Have you known people who didn't have one and had difficulties at the end of their lives as a result?

16. Erickson writes that she believes funerals are for the living, not the deceased. Do you agree? What rituals would you like at the end of your life, if any?

17. What cultural differences have you observed in relation to end-of-life issues and customs?

18. Of the people in Erickson's book, who do you think has the healthiest attitude toward death?

Notes

4   *"Well, you don't want to leave"*: Richard Rohr, "Finding God in the Depths of Silence," Festival of Faiths, Actors Theatre of Louisville, Louisville, Kentucky, May 15, 2013.

16   *"I have not mistreated cattle" and other selections from Egyptian rituals:* Don Nardo, *Mummies, Myth, and Magic: Religion in Ancient Egypt* (Detroit, MI: Lucent Books, 2005), 51, 55.

33   *"I am of the nature to grow old"*: Thich Nhat Hanh and the Monks and Nuns of Plum Village, *Plum Village Chanting and Recitation Book* (Berkeley, CA: Parallax Press, 2000), 35.

35   *"Although it becomes a little bit harder to do"*: Kathleen Dowling Singh, *The Grace in Aging: Awaken as You Grow Older* (Boston: Wisdom Publications, 2014), 2.

58   *"To contemplate dying each day calls forth"*: Kathleen Dowling Singh, *The Grace in Dying: How We Are Transformed Spiritually as We Die* (San Francisco: HarperSanFrancisco, 1998), 22.

62   *"Dying is safe"*: Singh, *Grace in Dying*, 1–2.

63   *"Americans receive some of the best health care"*: Angelo E. Volandes, MD, *The Conversation: A Revolutionary Plan for End-of-Life Care* (New York: Bloomsbury, 2015), 26.

67   *"When we enter meditation"*: Cynthia Bourgeault, *Centering Prayer and Inner Awakening* (Lanham, MD: Cowley Publications, 2004), 81.

70   *"There comes a moment"*: Bourgeault, *Centering Prayer and Inner Awakening*, 81.

100   *"I am Resurrection and I am Life"*: The *Book of Common Prayer according to the Use of the Episcopal Church* (New York: Church Publishing, 1979), 491.

129   *"From the 1870s through the turn of the century"*: John Gurda, *Cream City Chronicles: Stories of Milwaukee's Past* (Madison: Wisconsin Historical Society Press, 2007), 149–50.

152 *"No man is an island":* John Donne, *Devotions upon Emergent Occasions Together with Death's Duel* (Ann Arbor: University of Michigan Press, 1959), 63.

155 *"And even you, most gentle death":* Francis of Assisi, "All Creatures of Our God and King," in *The Hymnal 1982 by the Episcopal Church* (New York: Church Publishing, 1985), no. 400, verse 6.

About the Author

From a childhood on an Iowa farm, Lori Erickson (www.lori erickson.net) grew up to become one of America's top travel writers specializing in spiritual journeys. She's the author of *Holy Rover: Journeys in Search of Mystery, Miracles, and God* and more than a thousand articles in publications that include *National Geographic Traveler, Woman's Day, Family Circle, Better Homes & Gardens, House Beautiful,* and the *Los Angeles Times.* She lives in Iowa City, Iowa, with her husband, Bob Sessions.